Gun Violence

Other Books of Related Interest:

Opposing Viewpoints Series
Social Justice

At Issue Series
Is Gun Ownership a Right?

Current Controversies Series
Guns and Violence

"Congress shall make
no law . . . abridging
the freedom of speech,
or of the press."

First Amendment to the U.S. Constitution

The basic foundation of our democracy is the First Amendment guarantee of freedom of expression. The Opposing Viewpoints Series is dedicated to the concept of this basic freedom and the idea that it is more important to practice it than to enshrine it.

Gun Violence

Louise I. Gerdes, Book Editor

GREENHAVEN PRESS
A part of Gale, Cengage Learning

Detroit • New York • San Francisco • New Haven, Conn • Waterville, Maine • London

GALE
CENGAGE Learning

Christine Nasso, *Publisher*
Elizabeth Des Chenes, *Managing Editor*

© 2011 Greenhaven Press, a part of Gale, Cengage Learning.

Gale and Greenhaven Press are registered trademarks used herein under license.

For more information, contact:
Greenhaven Press
27500 Drake Rd.
Farmington Hills, MI 48331-3535
Or you can visit our Internet site at gale.cengage.com

For product information and technology assistance, contact us at

Gale Customer Support, 1-800-877-4253
For permission to use material from this text or product, submit all requests online at
www.cengage.com/permissions

Further permissions questions can be emailed to permissionrequest@cengage.com

Articles in Greenhaven Press anthologies are often edited for length to meet page requirements. In addition, original titles of these works are changed to clearly present the main thesis and to explicitly indicate the author's opinion. Every effort is made to ensure that Greenhaven Press accurately reflects the original intent of the authors. Every effort has been made to trace the owners of copyrighted material.

Cover Image copyright iStockPhoto.com/alptrum.

LIBRARY OF CONGRESS CATALOGING-IN-PUBLICATION DATA

Gun violence / Louise I. Gerdes, book editor.
    p. cm. -- (Opposing viewpoints)
    Includes bibliographical references and index.
    ISBN 978-0-7377-4966-3 (hardcover) -- ISBN 978-0-7377-4967-0 (pbk.)
    1. Firearms and crime--Juvenile literature. 2. Gun control--Juvenile literature.
    3. Violent crimes--Juvenile literature. I. Gerdes, Louise I., 1953-
    HV7435.G862 2010
    364.2--dc22
                                                                    2010026764

Printed in the United States of America
1 2 3 4 5 6 7 14 13 12 11 10

Contents

Why Consider Opposing Viewpoints?   11

Introduction   14

Chapter 1: How Serious Is the Problem of Gun Violence?

Chapter Preface   22

1. Gun Violence Is a Serious Problem   25
   Andrew Goddard

2. The Link Between Gun Ownership   30
   and Gun Violence Is Flawed
   Jacob Deakins

3. The Flow of U.S. Guns Fuels Gun   41
   Violence in Mexico
   Tom Diaz

4. The Percentage of U.S. Guns Used in Mexican   50
   Gun Violence Is Exaggerated
   William P. Hoar

5. The Availability of Guns Increases the Risk   57
   of Suicide
   Matthew Miller and David Hemenway

6. The Availability of Guns Does Not   63
   Increase Suicide Rates
   Don B. Kates

7. Gun Violence Poses a Serious Threat to Children   69
   Marian Wright Edelman

8. Gun Safety Programs Reduce the Threat of   74
   Fatal Firearm Accidents Among Children
   *National Rifle Association-Institute
   for Legislative Action*

Periodical Bibliography   80

Chapter 2: What Factors Contribute to Gun Violence?

Chapter Preface   **82**

1. The Availability of Guns Increases   **85**
   Gun Violence
   Bob Herbert

2. Making Guns Less Available Does Not   **90**
   Reduce Gun Violence
   John R. Lott Jr.

3. Pro-Gun Organization Policies Promote   **94**
   Gun Violence
   John E. Rosenthal

4. Gun Violence Is a Symptom of Other   **98**
   Social Problems
   Courtland Milloy

5. Hate and Extremist Groups Encourage   **103**
   Gun Violence
   Astrid Dorélien, Michael Miller, and Peter Brody

6. Popular Culture Promotes Gun Violence   **116**
   Dariusz Dziewanski

7. America's Violent Culture Advances   **127**
   Gun Violence
   Andrew Stephen

Periodical Bibliography   **132**

Chapter 3: Do Private Gun Ownership Policies Reduce Gun Violence?

Chapter Preface   **134**

1. Laws Controlling Private Gun Ownership   **136**
   Will Reduce Gun Violence
   Brady Campaign to Prevent Gun Violence

2. Laws Controlling Private Gun Ownership Reduce   147
Its Deterrent Effect on Gun Crime
Robert A. Levy

3. College Campuses Are Safer Without   155
Concealed Weapons
Students for Gun Free Schools

4. College Campuses Are Less Safe Without   167
Concealed Weapons
Students for Concealed Carry on Campus

5. Laws Allowing Citizens to Carry   179
Concealed Weapons in National Parks
Will Make Visitors Safer
Clair Schwan

6. Allowing Citizens to Carry Concealed Weapons   185
in National Parks Is Dangerous
Dianne Feinstein

Periodical Bibliography   189

Chapter 4: What Laws and Regulations Should Govern Guns?

Chapter Preface   191

1. The Second Amendment Guarantees the Right   193
to Private Gun Ownership
Don B. Kates

2. Judicial Activism Wrongly Established a Second   200
Amendment Right to Private Gun Ownership
Dennis A. Henigan

3. Gun Show Loopholes Should Be Closed   207
City of New York

4. Background Checks at Gun Shows   214
Are Unnecessary
*National Rifle Association-Institute
for Legislative Action*

5 The Assault Weapons Ban Should Be Reinstated   **221**
     Delaware County Daily Times

6. The Assault Weapons Ban Should   **226**
     Not Be Reinstated
     Steven Warrick

Periodical Bibliography   **230**

For Further Discussion   **231**

Organizations to Contact   **235**

Bibliography of Books   **242**

Index   **245**

Why Consider Opposing Viewpoints?

> *"The only way in which a human being can make some approach to knowing the whole of a subject is by hearing what can be said about it by persons of every variety of opinion and studying all modes in which it can be looked at by every character of mind. No wise man ever acquired his wisdom in any mode but this."*
>
> John Stuart Mill

In our media-intensive culture it is not difficult to find differing opinions. Thousands of newspapers and magazines and dozens of radio and television talk shows resound with differing points of view. The difficulty lies in deciding which opinion to agree with and which "experts" seem the most credible. The more inundated we become with differing opinions and claims, the more essential it is to hone critical reading and thinking skills to evaluate these ideas. Opposing Viewpoints books address this problem directly by presenting stimulating debates that can be used to enhance and teach these skills. The varied opinions contained in each book examine many different aspects of a single issue. While examining these conveniently edited opposing views, readers can develop critical thinking skills such as the ability to compare and contrast authors' credibility, facts, argumentation styles, use of persuasive techniques, and other stylistic tools. In short, the Opposing Viewpoints Series is an ideal way to attain the higher-level thinking and reading skills so essential in a culture of diverse and contradictory opinions.

In addition to providing a tool for critical thinking, Opposing Viewpoints books challenge readers to question their own strongly held opinions and assumptions. Most people form their opinions on the basis of upbringing, peer pressure, and personal, cultural, or professional bias. By reading carefully balanced opposing views, readers must directly confront new ideas as well as the opinions of those with whom they disagree. This is not to simplistically argue that everyone who reads opposing views will—or should—change his or her opinion. Instead, the series enhances readers' understanding of their own views by encouraging confrontation with opposing ideas. Careful examination of others' views can lead to the readers' understanding of the logical inconsistencies in their own opinions, perspective on why they hold an opinion, and the consideration of the possibility that their opinion requires further evaluation.

Evaluating Other Opinions

To ensure that this type of examination occurs, Opposing Viewpoints books present all types of opinions. Prominent spokespeople on different sides of each issue as well as well-known professionals from many disciplines challenge the reader. An additional goal of the series is to provide a forum for other, less known, or even unpopular viewpoints. The opinion of an ordinary person who has had to make the decision to cut off life support from a terminally ill relative, for example, may be just as valuable and provide just as much insight as a medical ethicist's professional opinion. The editors have two additional purposes in including these less known views. One, the editors encourage readers to respect others' opinions—even when not enhanced by professional credibility. It is only by reading or listening to and objectively evaluating others' ideas that one can determine whether they are worthy of consideration. Two, the inclusion of such viewpoints encourages the important critical thinking skill of objectively evaluating an author's credentials and bias. This evaluation will illuminate an author's reasons for taking a particular stance on an issue and will aid in readers' evaluation of the author's ideas.

It is our hope that these books will give readers a deeper understanding of the issues debated and an appreciation of the complexity of even seemingly simple issues when good and honest people disagree. This awareness is particularly important in a democratic society such as ours in which people enter into public debate to determine the common good. Those with whom one disagrees should not be regarded as enemies but rather as people whose views deserve careful examination and may shed light on one's own.

Thomas Jefferson once said that "difference of opinion leads to inquiry, and inquiry to truth." Jefferson, a broadly educated man, argued that "if a nation expects to be ignorant and free . . . it expects what never was and never will be." As individuals and as a nation, it is imperative that we consider the opinions of others and examine them with skill and discernment. The Opposing Viewpoints Series is intended to help readers achieve this goal.

David L. Bender and Bruno Leone,
Founders

Introduction

> *"There seems to us no doubt, on the basis of both text and history, that the Second Amendment conferred an individual right to keep and bear arms."*
>
> —Justice Antonin Scalia,
> from the majority opinion in
> District of Columbia v. Heller

> *"The [Supreme] Court would have us believe that over 200 years ago, the Framers [of the Constitution] made a choice to limit the tools available to elected officials wishing to regulate civilian uses of weapons. . . . I could not possibly conclude that the Framers made such a choice."*
>
> —Justice John Paul Stevens,
> dissenting opinion in
> District of Columbia v. Heller

On June 26, 2008, the U.S. Supreme Court recognized what had long been a minority interpretation of the Second Amendment to the U.S. Constitution. For more than sixty years following the Court's 1939 decision in *United States v. Miller*, which upheld convictions under a 1934 statute that criminalized possession of unregistered sawed-off shotguns, federal courts ruled that the scope of the Second Amendment was limited to protecting the right of states to organize militias. In its controversial 5–4 decision in *District of Columbia v. Heller*, however, the Court for the first time acknowledged an individual right to own and possess guns. In his majority opinion striking down a 1976 District of Columbia handgun ban, Justice Antonin Scalia argued that the Second Amendment established an individual right for "law-abiding, responsible citizens to use arms in defense of hearth and home."[1] In his dissenting opinion, however, Justice John Paul Stevens lamented that the ruling overturned a "settled understanding" that the Second Amendment allowed regulation of civilian gun ownership and use. Thus, despite the Supreme Court ruling, the debate over the interpretation of the Second Amendment continues. The modern Second Amendment debate began when, in response to growing concern over gun violence, the federal government enacted increasingly strict gun control laws that limited gun ownership and possession. Indeed, the development of the individual right interpretation of the Second Amendment from a minority view to a right established by the U.S. Supreme Court mirrors the development of the debates over the problem of gun violence.

Early in the twentieth century, only state laws restricted gun ownership and possession. Following the assassination of President John F. Kennedy on November 22, 1963, however, activists began to call for federal gun control laws. Lee Harvey Oswald, it was discovered, had purchased through the mail the rifle that killed the president, which, activists argued, made the crime an interstate concern. Thus, they reasoned, the prohibition of mail-order gun sales was within the purview of Congress. Congress, however, did not act until the murders of Martin Luther King Jr. and Senator Robert F. Kennedy in 1968. That same year, Congress passed the Gun Control Act, which banned mail-order gun sales, prohibited most interstate guns sales, and barred possession by felons, fugitives, alcoholics, drug users, mental defectives, or juveniles. The gun control movement did not become organized, however, until the 1970s. During this decade, public fears over the growing problem of urban gun crime began to rise. Gun crime victim Mark Borinsky, along with Pete Shields—whose son

---

1. *District of Columbia v. Heller*, 554 U.S. 290 (2008).

was murdered during San Francisco's "Zebra" murders in 1973–74—formed the first gun control organization, the National Council to Control Handguns. Citing the connection between growing gun crime and the proliferation of guns in the United States, the gun control movement began its fight for increasingly stronger restrictions on gun ownership and possession.

The individual right interpretation of the Second Amendment emerged as a reaction to the Gun Control Act of 1968 and the growing political influence of the gun control movement. The National Rifle Association of America (NRA), originally formed as a shooting association, led the fight. When leadership in the early 1970s endorsed some gun control, however, NRA members became bitterly divided. In 1977, the NRA ousted the old leadership, turning the NRA into a single-issue group known as the gun lobby. In the late 1970s and early 1980s, the NRA and other gun owner organizations vehemently opposed any restrictions on gun ownership, citing the individual right interpretation of the Second Amendment. These advocates argue that if law-abiding citizens are prevented from owning guns, only criminals will have guns. They claim that gun control will not reduce gun violence. In fact, they reason, gun control makes it impossible for law-abiding citizens to defend themselves against gun crime. Rather than restrict gun ownership among law-abiding citizens, the gun lobby argues, to reduce gun violence, Congress should increase sentences for possession of firearms by criminals. Congress did so in 1984 when it passed the Armed Career Criminal Act. In the late 1980s, advocates gained further support for gun rights with the passage of the Firearms Owners Protection Act of 1986, which allowed interstate gun sales if legal in the buyer's home state. The act also allowed licensed firearms dealers to sell guns at gun shows and prohibited a national gun registry. The once minority individual rights interpretation of the Second Amendment was gaining political strength.

Gun control advocates countered these gun lobby successes in the late 1980s and into the 1990s. Following the January 17, 1989, killing of five schoolchildren in Stockton, California, by a man armed with a semiautomatic assault rifle, Congress banned the import of assault weapons. In response to claims by the gun lobby that such a ban violates the Second Amendment right to own and possess arms, gun control advocates argue that those who wrote the Second Amendment did not mean to grant individuals the right to shoot innocent schoolchildren with assault weapons. In addition to the assault weapons ban, in response to increasing pressure from gun control advocates, Congress also established a National Instant Criminal Background Check System (NICS) in 1998. Federally licensed dealers are required to use NICS to determine whether a prospective purchaser should be prohibited from buying a firearm under the Gun Control Act of 1968.

While the NRA came to accept that NICS was an effective way to prevent criminals from obtaining guns, during the 1990s, some gun rights organizations continued to oppose any restrictions. Gun Owners of America (GOA) and like-minded gun rights organizations argue that restrictions will not prevent gun violence. The GOA contends that the system is inaccurate and that most criminals do not purchase guns legally. In response to claims that gun control will reduce the problem of horrific shooting sprees, gun rights advocates maintain that these crimes might have been prevented if law-abiding citizens had been allowed to carry concealed weapons, and throughout the decade, more and more states began to pass right-to-carry laws that allow law-abiding citizens to carry handguns.

While the NRA, the GOA, and other gun rights groups argued for the individual rights interpretation of the Second Amendment, from the 1960s through the mid 1980s, this view had no support in Supreme Court rulings or in the constitutional law community. In the late 1980s, however, the individual right interpretation began to garner scholarly support. In 1989, a liberal law professor, Sanford Levinson of the University of Texas Law School, argued that gun control advocates, including himself, needed to accept that the Second Amendment did set some constraints on government regulation of guns in his controversial law review article, "The Embarrassing Second Amendment." Signals of support also came from the Supreme Court. In his 1997 book, *A Matter of Interpretation: Federal Courts and the Law*, Justice Scalia adopted the individual right view. In addition, a federal appeals court for the first time found in 2001 that the Second Amendment guaranteed an individual right to possess firearms in *United States v. Emerson*. The U.S. Court of Appeals for the Fifth Circuit concluded, however, that domestic violence restrictions, designed to reduce domestic violence deaths, were a legitimate limitation on those rights. Despite having received formal notification from the George W. Bush administration of its support for the individual right view in 2002, the U.S. Supreme Court declined to hear *Emerson*. In the following year, however, six Washington, D.C., residents questioned the constitutionality of the city's handgun ban in *Heller*. When the U.S. Supreme Court agreed to hear the case in 2008, it received sixty friend-of-the-court briefs. A majority favored striking down the handgun ban. The Bush administration also urged the Court to recognize an individual right. A slim majority of the Court agreed. "It is not the role of this Court to pronounce the Second Amendment extinct,"[2] Scalia ruled.

Despite the Supreme Court's decision, the debate continues. Some gun rights advocates see the case as a victory for individual gun ownership rights. "Laws that serve no legitimate governmental purpose but merely serve to harass gun owners, laws that make gun owning difficult or expensive—those laws are going to be struck down,"[3] argues Alan Gura,

2. Ibid.
3. Quoted in Kenneth Jost, "Gun Rights Debates," *CQ Researcher*, October 31, 2008.

the lawyer who successfully represented the plaintiffs in *Heller*. Other gun rights supporters are less optimistic. Stephen Halbrook asserts, "It's not as though all the gun regulations in the country are going to go by the wayside."[4] Some gun control advocates agree. According to Dennis Henigan of the Brady Center to Prevent Gun Violence, "We're actually quite encouraged by comments that the majority made in the course of that decision offering some reassurance that some very broad categories of gun laws . . . are what the court called presumptively lawful."[5] In fact, in 2009 the U.S. Supreme Court held in *United States v. Hayes* that the Lautenberg Amendment, which prohibits anyone convicted of a misdemeanor domestic violence crime from possessing a gun, was a reasonable restriction on individual gun ownership rights. Other gun control advocates worry that the decision will erode gun control successes. According to Philip Cook, professor of economics and sociology at Duke University, "At this point it remains hard to say how far the Supreme Court and the federal circuit courts are going to push this."[6]

Indeed, whether gun laws effectively reduce gun violence or unnecessarily limit the individual right to own and possess guns remains a volatile issue in courts and legislative bodies nationwide. The impact of *Heller* remains to be seen. According to Akron University School of Law professor E. Stewart Moritz, "Each side sees [the other's position] as a slippery slope."[7] Thus, he reasons, for those on both sides of the gun debate, "every inch of ground is so hard-fought. They don't know how to stop."[8] The authors of the viewpoints in *Opposing Viewpoints: Gun Violence* contest as passionately these and other issues concerning the nature and scope of gun violence in the following chapters: How Serious Is the Problem of Gun

4. Ibid.
5. Ibid.
6. Ibid.
7. Ibid.
8. Ibid.

Violence? What Factors Contribute to Gun Violence? Do Private Gun Ownership Policies Reduce Gun Violence? and What Laws and Regulations Should Govern Guns?

CHAPTER 1

How Serious Is the Problem of Gun Violence?

Chapter Preface

Although the number of lives lost in school shootings are few when compared with the total number of gun deaths, school shootings so profoundly shock the nation that they inevitably renew the gun violence debate. Thus, one of several controversies concerning the seriousness of the problem of gun violence is whether school shootings pose a serious threat to children and young adults or are a rare occurrence subsequently used by activists as a tool to flame the gun rights debate.

On April 16, 2007, gunman Seung-Hui Cho killed 32 people on the campus of Virginia Tech University. Immediately following this tragedy—the worst mass school shooting in modern U.S. history—commentators on both sides of the gun control debate proclaimed gun violence in schools to be a problem serious enough to require action. "There's a universal agreement that we have a problem with gun violence in schools," argues the National Rifle Association of America's Andrew Arulanandam. "If you look at the reality today," Arulanandam asserts, "we protect our assets in our banks, we protect our airports, we protect special events more than we protect our children in our schools."[1] Despite Arulanandam's claim that people universally agree that school gun violence is a serious problem, how best to reduce gun violence in schools remains contentious. For example, some gun rights activists seek to lift bans on carrying concealed weapons on campuses. Larry Pratt of the gun rights group Gun Owners of America released a statement on the day of the Virginia Tech massacre demanding an end to the gun-free zone law. Conservative columnist Ann Coulter agrees, "The reason schools are consistently popular targets for mass murderers is precisely because

1. Quoted in Kenneth Jost, "Gun Violence," CQ Researcher, May 25, 2007.

of all the idiotic 'Gun-Free School Zone' laws."[2] Gun control advocates, many police groups, and campus law enforcement strongly disagree. Princeton University public safety director Steven Healy claims, "The only folks who should have firearms on a campus are those people who are sworn and authorized to protect and are duly trained to do that."[3]

Other analysts argue that while horrific, school shootings are rare events. Exaggerated media attention, they maintain, only fuels public fear. "Campuses are the safest places in America," alleges Florida State University criminology professor Gary Kleck. "Serious violence on campus is the exception to that rule,"[4] he asserts. The editors of the *Economist*, a British newsmagazine, suggest that there is no epidemic of gun violence in American schools. In fact, they report, "Violence in schools has fallen by half since the mid-1990s; children are more than 100 times more likely to be murdered outside the school walls than within them."[5] These commentators claim that fears of rising school gun violence stem from the extensive media coverage that often follows school shootings. Some experts, such as criminal justice professor James Alan Fox and criminology professor Jack Levin, contend that media attention and overzealous efforts to reduce school shootings may simply intensify the fear of some students. They contend that drawing attention to school shootings reminds others that violence is a way to solve their problems. They reason that knowing students better and helping them deal with their problems sooner is the best way to prevent future school shootings.

Whether gun violence in America's schools is a serious problem or exaggerated by the media remains controversial. The authors in the following chapter debate other controver-

2. Ann Coulter, "Let's Make America a 'Sad-Free Zone!'" *Human Events*, April 23, 2007.
3. Quoted in Kenneth Jost, "Gun Violence," *CQ Researcher*, May 25, 2007.
4. Ibid.
5. *Economist*, "Much to Mourn, Little to Learn," October 7, 2006.

sies concerning whether gun violence is a serious problem. These controversies in turn foster debate over how best to address gun violence in America's schools and society at large.

"If such a thing existed, then today the National Security Threat Level for gun violence would be at level RED, which would represent the highest level."

Gun Violence Is a Serious Problem

Andrew Goddard

Gun violence poses a serious threat to Americans, argues Andrew Goddard in the following viewpoint. In fact, he asserts, twenty times more people have died from gun violence in the six years following the terrorist attacks of September 11, 2001, than died that horrific day. Nevertheless, while much has been done to reduce the threat of terrorism, little has been done to reduce gun violence, Goddard maintains. To prevent further unnecessary loss of life, he reasons, people should consider gun control legislation. Goddard, whose son was wounded during the April 2007 mass shooting at Virginia Tech, is a member of the Million Mom March in Virginia.

As you read, consider the following questions:

1. What did Goddard learn about bullet wounds when his son was shot?

Andrew Goddard, "Testimony of a Virginia Tech Parent Before a Panel at George Mason University," FreedomStatesAlliance.com, June 2007. Reproduced by permission of the author.

2. What does the author believe is a serious indication of the problem with gun control in the United States?

3. According to the author, how long will the gun violence threat level remain RED in the United States?

My name is Andrew Goddard and [on April 16, 2007] my son Colin was shot four times in room 211 of Norris Hall at Virginia Tech [VT]. I stand before you today ready to take you to a place that no one else may choose, or be at liberty, to take you. I want you to sit beside me in the hospital room on that Monday night with my son.

The Bedside of a Gunshot Victim

I want you to look at him lying there with all the pipes, tubes and wires of modern medicine connected all over his body. I want you to listen to the beeps and whirs of the machines that are working to help his body overcome the multiple shots. I want you to look at his face and see perhaps your own child or a loved one and feel with me the helplessness of being a parent that can do nothing for their child at that moment. You will learn, as I did, that bullet wounds are not sewn shut, due to risk of infection, but left to bleed. I want you to watch, as I did, as blood oozes from the five holes in his body, soaking the dressings, his pillow and his bed sheets. You will learn, as I did, that bullet fragments lodged in his body are not routinely removed and that they will stay with him for life, as will the huge titanium rod driven down the full length of his femur to stabilize the fracture. I wanted to take you to that bedside to remind you of the suffering of the survivors; I will leave it to others more qualified than I to take you to the place from which the majority of the other victims will never return.

Starting that night, and for almost every day since, I have conducted my own internal investigation into the event, as

Did You Know?

On average, every day:

- 300 people in America are shot or killed with a gun.
- 85 people die from gun violence, 35 of them murdered.
- 215 people are shot, but survive their gun injuries.
- 67 children and teens are shot or killed with a gun.
- 9 children and teens die from gun violence.
- 57 children and teens are shot, but survive their gun injuries.

Brady Campaign to Prevent Gun Violence,
"Gun Violence Overview," 2010.

any parent would do. I asked myself a million times, how did this happen to my son and why? I still have no concrete answers other than that this awful tragedy was the direct result of the interaction between a deranged individual and two simple, efficient and readily available killing machines.

As to the motive for the actions of the killer, I have no idea, but the method that he used to carry out this heinous act is much easier to understand. Despite what others have said, my son and the other victims were not in the wrong place at the wrong time. My son was in the right place, a classroom of a well-respected university at 9:00 A.M. in the morning. What place could have been righter? Despite what others may tell you, the fact that [shooter Seung-Hui] Cho was able to purchase his weapons so easily is a serious indication of the problems that exist with gun control in our country and especially here in Virginia.

A Serious Threat

On September 11, 2001, al Qaeda terrorists carried out the most horrifying attack on US soil ever, killing more than 3000 people in several locations. The government sprung into action and we as a nation were warned about the imminent threat to our lives posed by al Qaeda. Many new laws and various pieces of legislation were enacted to keep us safe from this hideous threat. The government even installed a color-coded alert system to keep us informed about the level of threat that these terrorists pose. I believe it is currently yellow.

Since that same day in 2001 at least 60,000 of our fellow citizens have been killed in gun violence, which represents a rate of killing of more than 20 times . . . that inflicted by al Qaeda. A rate of killing that they could only dream about, yet we are still unable or unwilling to review our legislation on gun control.

Members of the panel, if such a thing existed, then today the National Security Threat Level for gun violence would be at level RED, which would represent the highest level, or in other words "absolute certainty of attack." At least the same number of our fellow citizens will die from gunfire today as died at VT on April 16th. Indeed the number may be considerably higher. Sadly the level was also RED the day before the VT attack, the day of that attack, the day after the attack and every single day since. It is red today, it will be red tomorrow and will remain that way until we come to our senses and take some concrete action to protect ourselves from this needless slaughter.

Investigating a Tragedy

Yesterday I visited VT and was given a tour of Norris Hall by one of the police officers [who] investigated the incident. I was very impressed by his knowledge and the professional way that he dealt with my questions. I also saw the first signs of changes that the university is making in light of the knowledge learned from the attack. One specific example was the replacement of the original bump bar door locks with new flush mounted locks that cannot readily be chained together to corral victims into a killing zone.

Why do I ask you to consider the fine details? It became clear to me yesterday that the difference between me sitting here with my son and me sitting with the other parents of the deceased victims can be measured not in yards or feet, but in fractions of an inch. The difference in response time that meant the difference between life or death can be measured not in hours or minutes, but in mere seconds!

You as a panel need to examine all the aspects of this tragedy, as the eyes of the world are on you. When you finally make your report, you will have the ears of the world too. Please examine the minutia of this event, but don't be afraid to look at the big picture items also. The future security of American campuses and other locations is in your hands.

> "[The] assertion that 'gun ownership
> and gun violence rise and fall together'
> is simply not correct."

The Link Between Gun Ownership and Gun Violence Is Flawed

Jacob Deakins

Studies show no significant link between gun ownership and gun crime, claims Jacob Deakins in the following viewpoint. Nevertheless, some physicians and public health officials promote this myth to manipulate public opinion in favor of gun control. In truth, Deakins argues, gun-free zones, where mass shootings often occur, eliminate any chance of resistance or self-defense. Gun ownership not only has benefits, he maintains, but the U.S. Supreme Court also has established the right to bear arms as a fundamental human right. Deakins is chief resident in the University of Wyoming Family Medicine Residency at Casper.

As you read, consider the following questions:

1. What example does Deakins provide to show how fear in the absence of fact has been used to manipulate opinion?

Jacob Deakins, "Guns, Truth, Medicine, and the Constitution," *Journal of American Physicians and Surgeons*, vol. 13, Summer 2008, pp. 58–60. Copyright © 2008 Association of American Physicians and Surgeons, Inc. Reproduced by permission.

2. What has proven to be more effective in reducing the harm caused by firearms than scare tactics?

3. What is the primary question to be answered by the U.S. Supreme Court in *District of Columbia v. Heller*?

"Medical inertia" is the term I use when something in medicine is blindly carried forward into the subsequent generations of physicians, despite a glaring lack of evidence-based research to support it.

As I read the perspective piece by Garen J. Wintemute, M.D., M.P.H., entitled "Guns, Fear, the Constitution, and the Public's Health" in the *New England Journal of Medicine*, two things came to mind: medical inertia and fearmongering.

Arguing from Fear

The author starts his article with a story about a foreign exchange student who mistakenly approached the incorrect house when trying to find a high school party, and was shot by a frightened homeowner. While this is undoubtedly a tragedy, it is an anecdote, not an argument, an appeal to fear rather than to reason.

Fear in the absence of fact has been used throughout history to manipulate opinion. In the Soviet Union, fear was used very effectively in propaganda, targeting even small children and adolescents. For example, a poster showing a very frightening skeleton-like figure under the wheels of a streetcar was captioned: "Remember that in 1925, 200 people died under the wheels of streetcars." This was aimed at children to prevent them from "ski bobbing"—holding on to the rear of the car and sliding on the ice during the frozen winter months. It was a very mild example of widely used methods.

Should physicians and public health officials be adopting this tactic? The Centers for Disease Control and Prevention (CDC) has done so for many years—at least on the issue of firearms. It was said that "'gun control'—which itself covers a variety of activities from registration to confiscation" was not the specific reason for the creation of the CDC's Intentional Injuries Section of the Division of Injury Epidemiology and Control. Its acting chief, Patrick O'Carroll, M.D., however, was quoted as saying that "[T]he way we're going to [achieve some form of regulation] is to systematically build a case that owning firearms causes death." Later, O'Carroll stated that he had been misquoted: "Such an approach would be anathema [a curse] to any unbiased scientific inquiry because it assumes the conclusion at the outset and then attempts to find evidence to support it." He asserted that "we at the CDC have been careful to avoid such a biased approach." Or should he have said "the appearance of bias"? It has been pointed out that he did not claim being misquoted in saying, "we are doing the most we can do, given the political realities."

The fearmongering has acquired medical inertia, as in the oft-cited myth of the relationship between legal gun ownership and murders and suicides. Wintemute simply asserts, without references, that gun owners have a 90% to 460% increased risk of dying by suicide, and a 40% to 170% risk of dying by homicide.

The Facts About Guns and Violence

Wintemute's assertion that "gun ownership and gun violence rise and fall together" is simply not correct. In an article for the *Harvard Journal of Law & Public Policy*, authors Don B. Kates, a criminologist at the Pacific Research Institute, and Gary Mauser, also a criminologist and professor at Simon Fraser University, British Columbia, asked whether banning firearms would reduce murder and suicide. They conclude:

> International evidence and comparisons have long been offered as proof of the mantra that more guns mean more death, and that fewer guns, therefore mean fewer deaths. Unfortunately, such discussions [have] all too often been afflicted by misconceptions and factual error, and focus on

comparisons that are unrepresentative. It may be useful to begin with a few examples. There is a compound assertion that (a) guns are more uniquely available in the United States, compared with other modern nations, which is why (b) the United States has by far the highest murder rate. Though these assertions have been endlessly repeated, statement (b) is in fact false, and statement (a) is substantially so.

Their findings are supported by multiple studies whose initial intent was to provide corroborating evidence to support banning firearms. For example, Professor Brandon Centerwall of the University of Washington compared Canada's more restrictive gun control policies to those of the United States, in order to determine whether Canadian policies had been more effective in curbing criminal violence. In an accompanying commentary, he states:

> If you are surprised by our findings, so are we. We did not begin this research with any intent to "exonerate" handguns, but there it is—a negative finding, to be sure, but a negative finding is nevertheless a positive contribution. *It directs us where not to aim our public health resources* [emphasis added].

The U.S. National Academy of Sciences in an extensive 2004 review of hundreds of journal articles, books, government publications, and original research failed to identify any evidence that gun control had reduced violent crime, suicides, or gun violence. The CDC had drawn a similar conclusion in a 2003 review of available research.

Despite all the data to the contrary, many choose to pursue the fear approach, realizing its effectiveness in many people at an emotional level. Who doesn't want to see fewer people harmed by firearms? While scare tactics may be attempted, education at an early age is proven to be more effective, and as physicians we should be first and foremost educators. Most pro-gun groups support youth education programs in gun safety, because they realize this is a far more effective approach.

The Benefits of Gun Ownership

Not only does Wintemute promulgate fear, he denies that gun ownership has benefits. He states that increased gun ownership does not correlate with decreased crime rates, and even declares that this claim has been discredited. Yet the evidence for benefit is very strong. John R. Lott Jr. reviewed the FBI's [Federal Bureau of Investigation's] yearly crime statistics for all 3,054 U.S. counties over 18 years (1977–1994), the largest national survey of gun ownership and state police documentation in illegal gun use. Some of his conclusions are:

- While neither state waiting periods nor the federal Brady Law [Brady Handgun Violence Prevention Act] is associated with a reduction in crime rates, *adopting concealed-carry gun laws cut death rates from public multiple shootings by 69 percent.*

- Allowing people to carry concealed weapons deters violent crime—without any apparent increase in accidental death. If states without right-to-carry laws had adopted them in 1992, about 1,570 murders, 4,177 rapes, and 60,000 aggravated assaults would have been avoided annually.

- Children 14 to 15 years of age are 14.5 times more likely to die from automobile injuries, five times more likely to die from drowning or fire and burns, and three times more likely to die from bicycle accidents than they are to die from gun accidents.

- When concealed-carry laws went into effect in a given county, murders fell by 8 percent, rapes by 5 percent, and aggravated assaults by 7 percent.

- For each additional year concealed-carry laws are in effect, the murder rate declines by 3 percent, robberies by more than 2 percent, and rape by 1 percent.

Wintemute focuses on recent shootings in our public places—neglecting to mention that most of these occurred in "gun free" zones, effectively eliminating any chance of resistance to thwart the intended mayhem. What more could someone bent on this type of act hope for?

Take the example of the December 5, 2007, Omaha mall shooting. The "gun free" zone even applied to the mall security guards, so there was no one to meet force with force, perhaps preventing further death. In the days that followed there were multiple Internet and blog postings by patrons of this mall. One such anonymous poster said:

> I am not allowed to carry a gun at all in Westroads Mall. If the laws did not oppress my rights ... I certainly would have had it in the mall. Honestly, and as God as my witness, when I saw him shooting and as I watched for a few seconds trying to figure out what he was going to do and what I should do, the thought that went through my head was, "If I had a gun, I have a perfect shot."

The next public shooting occurred on December 9 in Colorado. A man entered the Youth With A Mission training center and killed two, wounding two others. Several hours later he went to New Life Church in Colorado Springs. He murdered two sisters at the entrance, and was preparing to enter the building and campus, which was occupied by thousands at the time. He was met, however, by a member of the church's volunteer security force, Jeanne Assam, a private citizen who was armed with her handgun. She fired while being fired upon, and once the murderer was wounded he took his own life, likely sparing numerous other innocent lives.

In a recent *Detroit Free Press* article on Michigan's six-year-old right-to-carry law, and the assumption that more gun permit holders would equate to more gun deaths, a statement by a spokesman for the Michigan Association of Chiefs of Police is very illuminating:

> I think the general consensus out there from law enforcement is that things were not as bad as we expected. . . . I think we can breathe a sigh of relief that what we anticipated didn't happen.

The Second Amendment in the Courts

Current debate centers on a U.S. Supreme Court case, *District of Columbia v. Heller*.[1] This case stems from a 2003 federal lawsuit filed by six D.C. residents who argued that the District's gun ban infringed on their Second Amendment rights. The question is whether the Second Amendment refers to the so-called "collective right" of state governments to regulate their militias, or to an individual right of all citizens to "keep and bear arms."

Many medical organizations filed amicus briefs in this case, citing fear for the public's health and omitting any benefits of gun ownership. Like them, Wintemute sides with the District's interpretation that the Second Amendment only pertains [to] those who are in the service of a well-regulated militia, the modern-day equivalent of which is the National Guard. This contradicts multiple previous Supreme Court rulings, which have consistently held that there is an individual right.

One such case is *Scott v. Sandford*, heard in 1857, in which the Court ruled that a free black man could not be an American citizen. Writing for the majority, Chief Justice Roger Taney explained that as citizens, black men would have the "right to . . . full liberty of speech in public and private upon all subjects which [a state's] own citizens might meet; to hold public

---

1. In June 2008, in a 5–4 decision, the U.S. Supreme Court in *Heller* struck down a ban on handgun ownership in the District of Columbia and held that the Second Amendment granted the right to have a handgun in the home.

Is It Safe to Have a Gun in Your House?

A gun is a great way to protect your home and family, however its safety depends on the user. If members of the house are responsible and educated gun owners, then having a gun in the house will make it a safer place. A gun is significantly more likely to be used in defense of your home and family than be used in an irresponsible manner. Motor vehicle accidents, drowning, suffocation, and fires each kill more children under the age of fifteen than do firearms. If you think it is safe to have a bathtub in your house, then it is also safe to have a gun there.

Florida State University criminologist Gary Kleck reports that guns are used defensively about one million times per year. Ninety-eight percent of those times, not a single shot is fired, since the criminal runs away at the sight of the gun. Researcher John Lott, using fifteen surveys from such organizations as the *Los Angeles Times* and Gallup, concluded that guns were used defensively 760,000 to 3.6 million times. No matter which side you err on, that is a lot of defensive gun uses, definitely more than are hurt in gun violence in any year. In light of those statistics, the question changes into: Is it safe NOT to have a gun in your house?

Second Amendment Foundation,
"Frequently Asked Questions," 2000–2010. www.saf.org.

meetings upon political affairs and to keep and carry arms wherever they went." It is evident in this statement that Taney includes the right to keep and bear arms along with other individual rights of citizenship, such as the right to free speech and the right to assemble, which are protected in the Bill of Rights.

United States v. Cruikshank was brought after a group of white rioters burned down a courthouse in Louisiana that was occupied by a group of armed blacks. Ku Klux Klan leader William Cruikshank was held responsible and was on trial for conspiracies to violate the rights of the blacks that had been granted in the Constitution, such as the right to assemble and to be armed for self-protection. The entire premise was the then-existent Enforcement Acts, which criminalized private conspiracies to violate civil rights.

The decision, handed down in 1876, held that Cruikshank had conspired to deprive the blacks of their rights. Of interesting note, the Court ruled that the Enforcement Acts were unconstitutional, but that Congress did have the power to interfere to prevent violations of civil rights. The Court held:

> The right of bearing arms for a lawful purpose is not a right granted by the Constitution. Neither is it in any manner dependent on that instrument for its existence. The Second Amendment declares that it shall not be infringed; but this means no more than it shall not be infringed by Congress ... leaving the people to look for their protection against any violation by their fellow citizens of the rights it recognizes, to what is called ... the powers which relate to merely municipal legislation. ...

A Fundamental Human Right

Thus, the Supreme Court's view was that the Second Amendment *protects* the right to bear arms, but did not *create* it; rather, it exists as a fundamental human right. There are many more cases to support this view, including *Robertson v. Baldwin*. This was a Thirteenth Amendment case, which raised the question of whether merchant seamen who had jumped ship could be forced back into service, or whether this constituted a form of slavery. The case's relevance to the Second Amendment concerns unwritten exceptions contained in the Bill of Rights:

The law is perfectly well settled that the first ten amendments to the Constitution, commonly known as the Bill of Rights, were not intended to lay down any novel principles of government, but simply to embody certain guarantees and immunities which we had inherited from our English ancestors, and which from time immemorial had been subject to certain well-recognized exceptions arising from the necessities of the case. In incorporating these principles into the fundamental law, there was no intention of disregarding the exceptions, which continue to be recognized as if they had been formally expressed. Thus, the freedom of speech and of the press (Article 1) does not permit the publication of libels, blasphemous or indecent articles, or other publications injurious to public morals or private reputation; the right of the people to keep and bear arms (Article 2) is not infringed by law prohibiting the carrying of concealed weapons; the provision that no person shall be twice put in jeopardy (Article 5) does not prevent a second trial, if upon the first trial the jury failed to agree, or the verdict was set aside upon the defendant's motion. . . . Likewise the self-incrimination clause did not bar the admission of dying declarations.

These 19th-century cases lay a solid foundation for an individual right to keep and bear arms. There are multiple cases in the 20th century that despite not directly involving the Second Amendment, do use it as a reference to support a whole view of individual rights.

The medical and public health case against the right to self-defense with firearms, as epitomized by Wintemute, is primarily based on fear, buttressed by repetition of unfounded assertions or biased statistics. Logic, however, dictates that risks be weighed against benefits, and that an objective, complete assessment be made. Moreover, the inestimable importance of protecting liberty and individual rights requires that certain risks must be taken. The fundamental natural right of individuals to keep and bear arms is recognized in historical

Supreme Court decisions, including some not specifically based on the Second Amendment.

> "It is beyond question that firearms from the U.S. civilian gun market are fueling violence not only on both sides of the U.S./Mexico border, but in Mexico itself."

The Flow of U.S. Guns Fuels Gun Violence in Mexico

Tom Diaz

Military-style weapons from the U.S. civilian gun market are fueling drug-war violence in Mexico, asserts Tom Diaz in the following viewpoint. In fact, he maintains, drug cartels obtain as much as 95 percent of their guns from the United States. Weak gun regulation and the legal sale of semiautomatic assault weapons in the United States makes reducing gun trafficking into Mexico difficult, Diaz claims. Thus, he reasons, to reduce border gun violence, the United States should stop the production of military-style guns and require background checks for all gun transfers. Diaz, a lawyer and former journalist, is a senior policy analyst for the Violence Policy Center.

Tom Diaz, "Statement Before the Subcommittee on National Security & Foreign Affairs, Committee on Oversight and Government Reform," U.S. House of Representatives hearing on, "Money, Guns, and Drugs: Are U.S. Inputs Fueling Violence on the U.S./Mexico Border?" March 12, 2009. Reproduced by permission of the author.

As you read, consider the following questions:

1. According to William J. Hoover of the ATF, what are the three primary source states of illegally trafficked U.S. firearms?

2. What percentage of the firearms used by Mexican drug cartels reportedly came from the United States?

3. What is not required for gun sales in secondary markets?

It is beyond question that firearms from the U.S. civilian gun market are fueling violence not only on both sides of the U.S./Mexico border, but in Mexico itself. If one set out to design a "legal" market conducive to the business of funneling guns to criminals, one would be hard-pressed to come up with a "better" system than the U.S. civilian gun market—short of simply and openly selling guns directly to criminals from manufacturer and importer inventories.

The U.S. gun market not only makes gun trafficking in military-style weapons easy. It practically compels that traffic because of the gun market's loose regulation and the gun industry's ruthless design choices over the last several decades.

The Drug Cartels' Weapons of Choice

Military-style weapons heavily marketed by the U.S. civilian gun industry are the drug cartels' weapons of choice.

One need look no further than the testimony of William J. Hoover, assistant director, Office of Field Operations, Bureau of Alcohol, Tobacco, Firearms and Explosives (ATF), before the Western Hemisphere Subcommittee of the U.S. House of Representatives Committee on Foreign Affairs in February 2008 to find confirmation of that fact:

Mexican drug trafficking organizations have aggressively turned to the U.S. as a source of firearms. These weapons are used against other DTOs [drug trafficking organizations], the Mexican military, Mexican and U.S. law enforcement officials, as well as innocent civilians on both sides of the border. Our comprehensive analysis of firearms traces data over the past three years [and] shows that Texas, Arizona, and California are the three primary source states respectively for U.S.-sourced firearms illegally trafficked into Mexico. *Recently, the weapons sought by drug trafficking organizations have become increasingly higher quality and more powerful. These include the Barrett .50-caliber rifle, the Colt AR-15 .223-caliber assault rifle, the AK-47 7.62-caliber assault rifle and its variants, and the FN 5.57-caliber pistols, better known in Mexico as the cop killer.* [Italics added.]

It is no coincidence that the military-style firearms identified by Mr. Hoover as favored by Mexican drug cartels—and cop-killing criminals in the United States—are *precisely* the makes and models of firearms that have been carefully designed, manufactured or imported, and heavily marketed over the last 20 years by the U.S. civilian gun industry. These types of military-style firearms today dominate the U.S. civilian market.

The Gap in U.S. Policy

Much U.S. policy attention in response to public safety concerns has been directed at changing *internal* factors in Mexico and other key Latin American states to achieve transparency and effective policing within the rule of law. Less attention has been given to examining and correcting *external* influences from the United States that are driving much of the violence in Mexico and elsewhere in the Western Hemisphere. This gap in analytical thinking has sometimes contributed to myopic [nearsighted], piecemeal, and ultimately ineffective policies.

One of the major drivers in Mexico's violence that has been ignored until recently is the illicit flow of weapons to criminal organizations from the U.S. civilian firearms market.

Moreover, to the extent that the problem of gun trafficking has been addressed, the focus has been exclusively on law enforcement measures—investigating, identifying, and prosecuting gun smugglers. Although aggressive law enforcement measures are an essential part of any effective overall program, an exclusive focus on law enforcement measures overlooks a rich and ultimately more fruitful range of prophylactic [preventive] measures that can be implemented upstream of the transfers that move firearms from legal to illegal commerce.

The Role of the U.S. Gun Industry

"There is a war going on on the border between two cartels," William Newell, Special Agent in Charge of ATF's Phoenix Field Division, was reported to have said in 2007. "What do they need to fight that war? Guns. Where do they get them? From here." This statement of fact is not surprising. The VPC [Violence Policy Center] has reported in detail previously that it is entirely possible to outfit an army through the *civilian* commerce in firearms and related accessories in the United States. That is what the Mexican DTOs are doing today. According to ATF Special Agent Tom Mangan, "The cartels are outfitting an army."

Smugglers reportedly move guns into Mexico in a variety of ways, but according to the Associated Press, "most are driven through ports of entry, stuffed inside spare ties, fastened to undercarriages with zip ties, kept in hidden compartments, or bubble-wrapped and tucked in vehicle panels." Arizona's Attorney General [Terry Goddard] described this traffic recently as "a 'parade of ants'—it's not any one big dealer, it's lots of individuals." The dimensions of that traffic are not known, but it appears to be growing. U.S. and Mexican officials report that, based on ATF tracing data, the cartels get between 90 percent and 95 percent of their firearms from the United States. Traces by ATF of firearms from Mexico have reportedly increased from 2,100 in 2006 to 3,300 in 2007 and 7,700 in 2008.

Such information illustrates graphically that if one set out to design a system for easily moving military-style firearms from legal civilian commerce to illegal trade through gun smuggling, one could not do better than the existing U.S. civilian firearms market. The hallmarks of that trade not only make gun-running of the cartels' military-style weapons of choice easy, but very nearly compel this illicit commerce. Those hallmarks are:

1. Lax laws and regulations governing the firearms industry at the local, state, and federal levels, compounded by weak or ineffective enforcement.

2. The deliberate choice of military-style firearms design— assault weapons, .50-caliber anti-armor sniper rifles, and "vest-busting" handguns—by gun manufacturers and importers. Heavy industry marketing of these designs has made them the defining products in the U.S. civilian gun market today.

Lax Law and Regulation, Weak Enforcement

Although the gun lobby often maintains that the firearms industry is heavily regulated, in fact the industry is lightly regulated. The most important regulatory burdens on the gun industry are largely exercises in paper oversight—pro forma [done as only a formality] licensing and rare inspections by federal authorities. Most states do not regulate dealers, and the few that do rarely conduct regular inspections. Firearms and tobacco products are the only consumer products in the United States that are not subject to federal health and safety regulation. The sale (transfer) of firearms is subject only to a cursory federal background check under the federal Brady

Law [Brady Handgun Violence Prevention Act]—when the sale is made through a federally licensed gun dealer.

One of the most important problems in preventing domestic and foreign gun smuggling alike is that—unlike illegal drugs, for example—firearms are not inherently contraband. Guns enter into commerce legally and may be legally transferred in a wide variety of ways in a multitude of venues. The act of transferring a semiautomatic assault rifle—or a dozen—in entirely legal commerce between two law-abiding individuals is almost always indistinguishable from weapons transfers in which one or both of the parties intend to put the gun into the smuggling stream.

Oversight of firearm transfers quickly dissipates the further down the distribution chain one goes. Many of the ways that guns legally change hands in the United States are wholly unregulated and invisible from public view. These include, for example, sales by non-dealers at gun shows and sales between individuals.

The structure of the gun industry is relatively simple. Domestic and foreign manufacturers make the firearms. Domestically manufactured or assembled firearms are distributed by the manufacturers, either through wholesalers (known in the industry as "distributors") or directly to retail gun dealers. Foreign-made firearms are brought into the country through importers and then enter the same channels of commerce. In theory, imported firearms are required to have a "sporting purpose" under 18 USC §925(d)(3) (a provision of the 1968 Gun Control Act). In practice, however, the "sporting purposes" test is subject to administrative interpretation as to its definition and its application in specific cases. Under the George W. Bush administration, the sporting purposes test was substantially weakened, allowing the importation of a large number of cheap assault weapons and such "cop-killing" handguns as the FN Five-seveN, known in Mexico as the *mata policia*, or "cop killer."

A Weak System

Domestic firearm manufacturers, importers, dealers, and ammunition manufacturers are required to obtain a Federal Firearms License (FFL). This licensing regimen effects the central purpose of the Gun Control Act of 1968, the core federal gun law, of supporting state control of firearms by basically forbidding interstate commerce in guns except through federally licensed dealers. However, FFLs are issued on a virtually pro forma basis—anyone who is at least 21 years old, has a clean arrest record, nominal business premises, and agrees to follow all applicable laws can get a license good for three years upon paying a fee and submitting a set of fingerprints with an application form.

New and imported firearms thus in theory always move in legal commerce through at least one federally licensed seller through the first retail sale. The federal Brady Law requires a background check as a prerequisite to any retail sale *through a*

47

federally licensed dealer. However, once a gun has been sold at retail, it may be resold in the "secondary market"—that is, not through a federally licensed dealer—any number of times using any one of a variety of channels. Vehicles for these secondary market transfers include classified advertising in newspapers and newsletters, Internet exchanges, and informal sales between individuals at "flea markets" or "gun shows." None of these secondary market channels require the federal Brady background check, so long as the sale is conducted intrastate and there is no state background check requirement. Most states do not regulate such sales—although a few, like California, do regulate all firearms transfers. About 40 percent of all gun transfers are made through this secondary market, according to a 1994 national survey.

The consequences of this weak system are apparent in the fact that domestic gun trafficking is widespread and resistant to such law enforcement efforts as exist. Street gangs and other criminal organizations have demonstrated conclusively over the last 25 years that weak U.S. gun control laws do not prevent their acquiring as many of the increasingly lethal products of the gun industry as they desire. In spite of episodic efforts by ATF, organized interstate smuggling pipelines continue to move guns from states with virtually nonexistent gun regulations to the few primarily urban centers that have tried to stem the flow of guns. "States that have high crime gun export rates—i.e., states that are top sources of guns recovered in crimes across state lines—tend to have comparatively weak gun laws." Local criminals engage in brisk gun traffic in every part of the country, with little effective law enforcement interference.

Some opponents of more effective gun control measures point to the continued trade in illegal firearms as evidence that the gun control laws do not work. "A crook could care less how many laws you have," a border region gun dealer told the *Los Angeles Times* in 2008. Former Secretary of State Condoleezza Rice was reported by *El Universal* newspaper to have made a similar statement at a meeting with Mexico's Foreign [Affairs] Secretary, Patricia Espinosa. "I follow the traffic in arms throughout the world, and I have never known traffickers in illegal arms to care much about the law," the paper quoted Rice as saying. Based on the logic that laws do not deter criminals, the newspaper dryly observed, Mexico should repeal its laws against drug trafficking.

In fact, the major weakness of U.S. efforts against gun trafficking (and firearms violence in general) is its almost total reliance on after-the-fact law enforcement investigation and prosecution. Instead of focusing on prophylactic measures to prevent guns from getting into the hands of traffickers, most attention has been paid to trying to apprehend and prosecute traffickers after the damage has been done and the guns are in criminal hands. If, as noted earlier, traffickers indeed use a "stream of ants" to move guns to Mexico, it would be more effective to focus efforts on making it more difficult for the ants to get the guns in the first place.

Although law enforcement efforts are an important and necessary part of a total package against gun trafficking—and gun violence generally—a more powerful solution would be to complement law enforcement with "upstream" public health and safety measures designed to reduce the opportunity for gun trafficking. Examples of these upstream measures include stopping the production and import of military-style firearms such as semiautomatic assault weapons and .50-caliber anti-armor sniper rifles, and making all transfers of firearms subject to (at a minimum) the current background check to which transfers through federally licensed firearms dealers are subject.

Even if the commerce in firearms in the United States were more tightly regulated along such lines, there remains the major problem of lack of oversight over design—the type of firearms that the gun industry produces and markets.

> "The percentage of guns recovered at Mexican crime scenes originating in the United States—is being sprayed around like real machine-gun fire. Very inaccurately, as it turns out."

The Percentage of U.S. Guns Used in Mexican Gun Violence Is Exaggerated

William P. Hoar

Gun control advocates exaggerate the number of U.S. guns found at Mexican drug-war crime scenes, claims William P. Hoar in the following viewpoint. Officials base the inflated number on traced guns, which comprise only a small portion of the actual number of guns used by drug cartels, he maintains. Most of the guns actually come from other countries in Central and South America and from those who have deserted the Mexican military, Hoar argues. Gun opponents overstate gun numbers to promote greater gun control and to reinstate the assault weapons ban, he reasons. Hoar writes for the John Birch Society, a conservative organization that supports limited government.

William P. Hoar, "Mexican Violence, Gun Controls," *New American*, vol. 25, May 25, 2009, pp. 42–43. Copyright © 2009 American Opinion Publishing Incorporated. Reproduced by permission.

As you read, consider the following questions:

1. In what areas does Hoar say the worst shooting incidents in the United States have occurred?

2. What percentage of the guns recovered by the Mexican government were never submitted for tracing, according to Fox News reporters?

3. What nation made the M16s that 150,000 Mexican military deserters took with them?

Item: On the CBS television show *Face the Nation* on April 12 [2009], in an interview with Bob Schieffer, Mexico's Ambassador to the United States Arturo Sarukhán tried to blame much of the violence in his country on the allegedly lax gun control laws in the United States. He maintained in part: "Ninety percent of all weapons we are seizing in Mexico, Bob, are coming from across the United States." Reinstituting the so-called assault-weapons ban in the United States, which expired in 2004, said the ambassador, "could have a profound impact on the number and the caliber of weapons going down to Mexico."

Item: On April 20, *Time* magazine commemorated the 10th anniversary of the murders at Columbine High School in Littleton, Colorado, with an article on its Time.com site decrying that, over the past decade, "massacres perpetrated by deranged gunmen have continued." However, said writer Michael Lindenberger, "something odd has occurred. Whatever momentum the Columbine killings gave to gun control has long since petered out." The *Time* writer grumbled that "the debate seems to be almost one-sided nowadays, with an ongoing backlash against gun control."

Correcting Misconceptions

Correction: The *Time* writer who complained about one-sidedness in the gun control "debate" was firing blanks: He gave but one side of the issue—for more controls.

As it happens, the worst shooting incidents in the United States have occurred in areas where the deck has been stacked against armed self-defense. As pointed out by John [R.] Lott [Jr.], a senior research scientist at the University of Maryland and the author of *More Guns, Less Crime,* "All multiple victim public shootings with more than three people killed have occurred where permitted concealed handguns are prohibited."

Meanwhile, the "90 percent" figure—widely alleged to be the percentage of guns recovered at Mexican crime scenes originating in the United States—is being sprayed around like real machine-gun fire. Very inaccurately, as it turns out.

For example, when President [Barack] Obama was in Mexico, he said: "More than 90 percent of the guns recovered in Mexico come from the United States, many from gun shops that lay in our shared border."

In similar fashion, Senator Dianne Feinstein, (D-Calif.) griped at a Senate hearing: "It is unacceptable to have 90 percent of the guns that are picked up in Mexico and used to shoot judges, police officers and mayors ... come from the United States."

Loaded Statistics and Overblown Figures

That loaded statistic has also been used by, among others, Mexican President Felipe Calderón, Secretary of State Hillary Clinton, the *Washington Post,* CNN, and innumerable other media outlets, and even an official from the Bureau of Alcohol, Tobacco, Firearms and Explosives (BATF) before Congress.

Yet, those figures are wildly overblown. When pressed by William La Jeunesse and Maxim Lott of Fox News, a spokeswoman for BATF acknowledged that "over 90 percent of the *traced* firearms originated from the United States—a very different figure." An analysis by Fox revealed that the statistic so favored by the gun grabbers referred only to a much smaller subtotal that Mexico sent to the United States and were successfully traced; it didn't include the thousands obviously not from the United States that were not submitted to the BATF. As the Fox writers explained:

> In 2007–2008, according to ATF Special Agent William Newell, Mexico submitted 11,000 guns to the ATF for tracing. Close to 6,000 were successfully traced—and of those, 90 percent—5,114 to be exact, according to testimony in Congress by William Hoover—were found to have come from the U.S.
>
> But in those same two years, according to the Mexican government, 29,000 guns were recovered at crime scenes.
>
> In other words, 68 percent of the guns that were recovered were never submitted for tracing. And when you weed out the roughly 6,000 guns that could not be traced from the remaining 32 percent, it means 83 percent of the guns found at crime scenes in Mexico could not be traced to the U.S.

A special agent for United States Immigration and Customs Enforcement (ICE) named Matt Allen informed Fox News that "the United States' effort to trace weapons really only extends to weapons that have been in the U.S. market." In other words, the statistics echoed by one gun control advocate after another are far wide of their mark, since the large number of weapons seized in Mexico from countries other than the United States were not included in the count.

Firing Back

Second Amendment supporters have been firing back at the phony barrage from the other side. Senator James Inhofe (R-Okla.), for instance, doesn't buy the contention that violence in Mexico justifies stripping Americans of our rights. Says the senator:

The majority of the gun violence that is occurring in the drug wars in Mexico is the result of assault weapons, including fully automatic versions, which aren't even available for sale in the United States. Many of these weapons are coming from other countries in Central and South America and deserters from the Mexican military.

The figure mentioned by Inhofe is a reference to the estimated 150,000 Mexican troops who have deserted in the past six years, many taking their Belgian-made M16s with them.

The violence in Mexico is being duplicitously used as ammunition by would-be gun controllers in this country. Attorney General Eric Holder is among these. He said not long ago that in order to quell the incidents on the border he would try to reinstate the so-called assault-weapons ban. The ban, since expired, on so-called assault weapons proved of no use in fighting crime. However, that never stops gun control proponents.

The "assault weapons" covered by the law were nothing of the sort, but merely had some features that looked like military weapons or a magazine that held more than 10 rounds. According to state and local police reports (as cited by the NRA's [National Rifle Association of America's] Institute for Legislative Action), "assault weapons" are used in about 1 percent of murders; by comparison, more than 30 percent of murders are committed with no firearms at all.

To its credit, *Face the Nation* did invite the executive director of the National Rifle Association to offer a rebuttal to the latest gun-ban move. Wayne LaPierre gave 'em both barrels. The legislation in 1994, as he made clear, "was enacted . . . on the basis of saying these were machine guns. That's a lie. They were rapid-fire. That's a lie. They made bigger holes. That's a lie. They were more powerful. That's a lie. It was lie after lie after lie," he said. Concluded LaPierre, "Congress found it out. That's why they let it expire."

An Assault on Rights

All the same, the Obama transition team admitted that "making the expired federal assault-weapons ban permanent" is a goal of the administration.

If you think the assault-weapon ban was a bizarre affront to your rights, take a look at the Blair Holt Act [Blair Holt's Firearm Licensing and Record of Sale Act of 2009, or H.R. 45], submitted by Representative Bobby Lee Rush (D-Ill.), who is among the more radical supporters of Barack Obama. The Rush legislation has been aptly summarized by columnist Paul Greenberg:

> H.R. 45 would oblige every gun owner in the country, after being thumb-printed and passing a government-approved training class, to obtain and carry a firearms license bearing passport-sized photo identification. In order to acquire that license, gun owners would have to prove that they have a government-approved storage place for their firearms. Each sale would be recorded by the U.S. government. The licensed gun owner would then face criminal prosecution if he failed to report every firearm he (or she) owns, or if said gun owner changed residence without informing the Attorney General of the United States, or if his firearm were stolen and the theft went unreported. As for you deer, duck or turkey hunters out there, this means, you, too. No exemptions.
>
> There's more, much more. There are so many sweeping provisions in this horse-choker of a bill, space doesn't permit citing all of them. H.R. 45 is almost Soviet in its sweep.

Rush is familiar with guns, after a fashion. The former Black Panther member spent six months in jail on a weapons charge.

Does this bill have a chance of passing? Not really. Freedom is more likely to be lost by inches, not by feet or yards.

However, such overreaching is useful to those pushing other gun grabs whose efforts will appear less radical by comparison.

"The empirical evidence linking suicide risk in the United States to the presence of firearms in the home is compelling."

The Availability of Guns Increases the Risk of Suicide

Matthew Miller and David Hemenway

Suicide is one of the risks of gun ownership, claim Matthew Miller and David Hemenway in the following viewpoint. Suicide is the second leading cause of death among young Americans, and more than half of the victims choose to use guns, they assert. Suicides are often impulsive acts based on a crisis that often passes, Miller and Hemenway maintain. Therefore, they argue, while many who choose less lethal means never go on to commit suicide, those who choose guns never have a chance to seek nonfatal alternatives to personal crises. Miller is the associate director and Hemenway is the director of the Harvard Injury Control Research Center at the Harvard School of Public Health.

As you read, consider the following questions:

1. How did deaths by suicide and homicide compare, according to 2005 mortality data?

2. What do studies show about suicide and how guns in the home are stored?

3. What have international experts concluded is an effective suicide-prevention policy?

This past June, in a 5-to-4 decision in *District of Columbia v. Heller*, the Supreme Court struck down a ban on handgun ownership in the nation's capital and ruled that the District's law requiring all firearms in the home to be locked violated the Second Amendment. But the Supreme Court's finding of a Second Amendment right to have a handgun in the home does not mean that it is a wise decision to own a gun or to keep it easily accessible. Deciding whether to own a gun entails balancing potential benefits and risks. One of the risks for which the empirical evidence is strongest,[1] and the risk whose death toll is greatest, is that of completed suicide.

In 2005, the most recent year for which mortality data are available, suicide was the second leading cause of death among Americans 40 years of age or younger. Among Americans of all ages, more than half of all suicides are gun suicides. In 2005, an average of 46 Americans per day committed suicide with a firearm, accounting for 53% of all completed suicides. Gun suicide during this period accounted for 40% more deaths than gun homicide.

Why might the availability of firearms increase the risk of suicide in the United States? First, many suicidal acts—one third to four fifths of all suicide attempts, according to studies—are impulsive. Among people who made near-lethal suicide attempts, for example, 24% took less than 5 minutes between the decision to kill themselves and the actual attempt, and 70% took less than 1 hour.[2]

Second, many suicidal crises are self-limiting. Such crises are often caused by an immediate stressor, such as the breakup of a romantic relationship, the loss of a job, or a run-in with police. As the acute phase of the crisis passes, so does the urge to attempt suicide. The temporary nature and fleeting sway of many suicidal crises is evident in the fact that more than 90% of people who survive a suicide attempt, including attempts that were expected to be lethal (such as shooting oneself in the head or jumping in front of a train), do not go on to die by suicide. Indeed, recognizing the self-limiting nature of suicidal crises, penal and psychiatric institutions restrict access to lethal means for persons identified as potentially suicidal.

Third, guns are common in the United States (more than one third of U.S. households contain a firearm) and are lethal. A suicide attempt with a firearm rarely affords a second chance. Attempts involving drugs or cutting, which account for more than 90% of all suicidal acts, prove fatal far less often.

The empirical evidence linking suicide risk in the United States to the presence of firearms in the home is compelling.[3] There are at least a dozen U.S. case-control studies in the peer-reviewed literature, all of which have found that a gun in the home is associated with an increased risk of suicide. The increase in risk is large, typically 2 to 10 times that in homes without guns, depending on the sample population (e.g., adolescents vs. older adults) and on the way in which the firearms were stored. The association between guns in the home and the risk of suicide is due entirely to a large increase in the risk of suicide by firearm that is not counterbalanced by a reduced risk of nonfirearm suicide. Moreover, the increased risk of suicide is not explained by increased psychopathologic characteristics, suicidal ideation, or suicide attempts among members of gun-owning households.

Three additional findings from the case-control studies are worth noting. The higher risk of suicide in homes with firearms applies not only to the gun owner but also to the gun owner's spouse and children. The presence of a gun in the home, no matter how the gun is stored, is a risk factor for completed suicide. And there is a hierarchy of suicide risk

Suicides in States with the Highest and Lowest Rates of Gun Ownership, 2001–2005

Variable	States with the Highest Rates of Gun Ownership	States with the Lowest Rates of Gun Ownership	Ratio of Mortality Rates
Percent of households with guns	47	15	—
Male			
No. of firearm suicides	14,365	3,971	3.7
No. of nonfirearm suicides	6,573	6,781	1.0
Total no.	20,938	10,752	2.0
Female			
No. of firearm suicides	2,212	286	7.9
No. of nonfirearm suicides	2,599	2,478	1.1
Total no.	4,811	2,764	1.8

TAKEN FROM: Matthew Miller and David Hemenway, *New England Journal of Medicine*, September 4, 2008.

consistent with a dose-response relationship. How household guns are stored matters especially for young people—for example, one study found that adolescent suicide was four times as likely in homes with a loaded, unlocked firearm as in homes where guns were stored unloaded and locked.

Many ecologic studies covering multiple regions, states, or cities in the United States have also shown a strong association between rates of household gun ownership and rates of completed suicide—attributable, as found in the case-control studies, to the strong association between gun prevalence and gun suicide, without a counterbalancing association between gun-ownership levels and rates of nongun suicide. We recently examined the relationship between rates of household gun ownership and suicide in each of the 50 states for the period between 2000 and 2002.[4] We used data on gun ownership from a large telephone survey (of more than 200,000 respondents) and controlled for rates of poverty, urbanization, unemployment, mental illness, and drug and alcohol dependence and abuse. Among men, among women, and in every age group (including children), states with higher rates of household gun ownership had higher rates of firearm suicide and overall suicides. There was no association between firearm-ownership rates and nonfirearm suicides. To illustrate the main findings, we presented data for the 15 states with the highest levels of household gun ownership matched with the six states with the lowest levels (using only six so that the populations in both groups of states would be approximately equal). In the table, the findings are updated for 2001 through 2005.

The recent Supreme Court decision may lead to higher rates of gun ownership. Such an outcome would increase the incidence of suicide. Two complementary approaches are available to physicians to help counter this possibility: to try to reduce the number of suicide attempts (e.g., by recognizing and treating mental illness) and to try to reduce the probability that suicide attempts will prove fatal (e.g., by reducing access to lethal means). Many U.S. physicians, from primary care practitioners to psychiatrists, focus exclusively on the first approach. Yet international experts have concluded that restriction of access to lethal means is one of the few suicide-prevention policies with proven effectiveness.[5]

In our experience, many clinicians who care deeply about preventing suicide are unfamiliar with the evidence linking guns to suicide. Too many seem to believe that anyone who is serious enough about suicide to use a gun would find an equally effective means if a gun were not available. This belief is invalid.

Physicians and other health care providers who care for suicidal patients should be able to assess whether people at risk for suicide have access to a firearm or other lethal means and to work with patients and their families to limit access to those means until suicidal feelings have passed. A Web site of the Harvard Injury Control Research Center can help physicians and others in this effort (www.hsph.harvard.edu/means-matter). Effective suicide prevention should focus not only on a patient's psychological condition but also on the availability of lethal means—which can make the difference between life and death.

Notes

1. Hemenway D. Private guns, public health. Ann Arbor: University of Michigan Press, 2004.
2. Simon OR, Swann AC, Powell KE, Potte LB, Kresnow MJ, O'Carroll PW. Characteristics of impulsive suicide attempts and attempters. Suicide Life Threat Behav 2001; 32:Suppl:49–59.
3. Miller M, Hemenway D. The relationship between firearms and suicide: a review of the literature. Aggress Violent Behav 1999;4:59–75.
4. Miller M, Lippmann SJ, Azrael D, Hemenway D. Household firearm ownership and rates of suicide across the 50 United States. J Trauma 2007;62:1029–35.
5. Mann JJ, Apter A, Bertolote J, et al. Suicide prevention strategies: a systematic review. JAMA 2005;294:2064–74.

> "If gun control eliminated gun suicide, the same suicides would occur by other means."

The Availability of Guns Does Not Increase Suicide Rates

Don B. Kates

The presence of a gun does not increase the risk of suicide, maintains Don B. Kates in the following viewpoint. If guns increase the risk of suicide, he argues, then studies would show a decrease in suicide rates in nations where guns are controlled or banned. In many studies, however, suicide rates in such nations have remained stable and in some cases have increased, Kates claims. People who are determined to end their lives will find a way to do so, he asserts. Kates, a criminologist and civil liberties lawyer, is coauthor, with criminologist Gary Kleck, of Armed: New Perspectives on Gun Control.

As you read, consider the following questions:

1. What public health view promotes the notion that guns increase suicide risk?

2. In what countries with high suicide rates have handguns always been banned?

Don B. Kates, "The Suicide and Gun-Deaths Fraud," *Handguns*, April–May 2006. Copyright © 2006 Intermedia Outdoors, Inc. Reproduced by permission.

3. What were the results of the Monash study that the
study's authors did not discuss?

The title ["The Suicide and Gun-Deaths Fraud"] is not
mine. I stole it from an article by Canadian criminologist
Gary Mauser, who teaches at British Columbia's Simon Fraser
University. That article appeared in the September 2005 *Fraser
Forum*. The "fraud" to which Prof. Mauser refers is studying
suicides committed with guns separately from other suicides
(as if the gun somehow caused the suicide), with the implica-
tion that banning the gun would have prevented the suicide.
But, Prof. Mauser writes, "It is demonstrably false that ordinary people are somehow motivated by the presence of a firearm to kill themselves or others. This paternalistic notion
stems from a public health view of people as 'patients' who
need treatment, and it is incompatible with the view that ordinary people are responsible citizens. By portraying the ordinary citizen as vulnerable, it is easier to justify government in-
tervention to protect us from ourselves."

He continues, "When people decide to commit suicide,
they naturally choose a method that will accomplish their
goals. Since guns are not uniquely more lethal than alternative
methods—e.g., hanging—one would expect that removing
firearms would not eliminate other effective alternatives. And
that is what is observed. Over the past decade in Canada, as
firearms have fallen out of fashion as a method of ending
one's life, hanging has increased in popularity, almost dou-
bling in frequency since 1995. The net result is that the suicide rate in Canada has remained relatively stable over the
past 10 years, declining very slightly from 13 to 12 per 100,000
population. If reduced access to guns is indeed responsible for
the decline in suicides involving firearms, it has not saved any
lives. Unfortunately, determined people still manage to find
ways to end their own lives."

Looking at the Evidence

His evidence for this includes his table "Methods of Suicide, Canada, 2001:"

Hanging	1,509	41%
Poisoning	968	26%
Shooting	651	18%
Jumping	264	7%
Drowning	106	3%
Sharp object	94	3%
Other	96	3%

In fact, though the U.S. suicide rate is higher than our murder rate, the suicide rates of other developed nations are higher yet, often much higher. The latest comprehensive international figures I have date from the late 1990s when the American suicide rate was 11.6 deaths per 100,000 people. By way of comparison, here are some other nations' suicide rates:

Germany, 15.8; Belgium, 18.7; France, 20.8; Switzerland, 21.4; Austria, 22.2; Denmark, 22.3; Finland, 27.2; Hungary, 32.9.

Far from handgun ownership correlating with high suicide rates, handguns are either illegal or severely restricted in both Denmark and Hungary. Suicide rates are even higher in three nations where handguns have always been banned—Russia (41.2) and the former Soviet nations Estonia (40.1) and Lithuania (45.6).

Mauser also notes that "overall Canadian suicide rates are higher than those in the U.S. despite the greater availability of guns in the U.S.," something that would be "unlikely if overall suicide rates were driven primarily by the availability of firearms. It is simplistic to think that suicide hinges upon the availability of any single method. Suicide patterns arise from a variety of depressing personal or social conditions. Unfortunately, such conditions exist in Canada, as well as in the United States."

Confusing Public Health Policies

Despite the ready (indeed overwhelming) availability of such evidence, credulous public health publications continue to insist that "limiting access to firearms could prevent many suicides." That opinion I take from a work by several of the most prolific and influential anti-gun public health writers. They actually cited as supporting that opinion an empirical study expressly finding the opposite, i.e. that if suicidal individuals do not have guns, they just turn to other methods of killing themselves. Thus, what the study actually said is that if gun control eliminated gun suicide, the same suicides would occur by other means.

Those who are interested in an extended discussion of these issues will find it in chapter two of my book (with criminologist Gary Kleck) *Armed: New Perspectives on Gun Control* (Prometheus, 2001).

Let me add a couple of later examples. In 2004 some anti-gun public health professors at Australia's Monash University published a study of the effect upon gun deaths of anti-gun laws in the state of Victoria. Though gun deaths had been declining in Australia for many years before Victoria adopted these laws, the study claimed they accelerated the decline, stating, "We estimate that if pre-1988 trends had continued in Australia, more than 1,000 more lives would have been lost to firearms."

Misleading Claims

This statement is highly misleading, tending as it does to deceive readers into thinking that the anti-gun laws resulted in 1,000 fewer deaths. Not true. For reasons best known to its authors, the Monash study did not discuss the real issue, which is whether anti-gun laws actually reduced murder and suicide. Only a reader alert to this real issue would see the significance of the study's brief and downplayed admission that despite the "declines related to [gun] homicide, overall suicide and homicide rates in Victoria did not show a similar decline." In other words, *gun* deaths fell, but murders and suicides by other deadly means just rose to make up the difference.

In 2002 Oxford University Press published *Can Gun Control Work?* by New York University [NYU] Prof. James Jacobs, who is also director of NYU's Center for Research in Crime and Justice. (The book is superb; Jacobs's answer as to banning handguns or all guns is "no," that will not work.)

One study Jacobs discusses sought to determine if the Brady Act [Brady Handgun Violence Prevention Act] reduced murder and/or suicide. To determine that, the study compared murder and suicide trends in the states that were under Brady to the trends in the states that were not subject to the federal Brady restrictions on handgun sales. Jacobs notes, "The statistical analysis provided 'no evidence that implementation of the Brady Act was associated with a reduction in homicide rates.' There was no statistical difference in homicide and suicide in Brady and [non-Brady] states, and the rate of suicide by handgun decreased in [Brady] states. . . . Nevertheless, there was no difference in total suicides in [Brady] and control states. In other words, if the Brady Act did have the effect of modestly reducing firearms suicides . . . this effect was completely offset by an increase of the same magnitude in nonfirearm suicide resulting in the same number of deaths."

The world is full of deadly mechanisms with which those who desire to kill others or themselves can do so. All that is accomplished by subtraction of one deadly means is that people will kill by some other means.

In considering this it is important to understand a further point. There is one crucial difference between guns and other kinds of deadly weapons. That crucial difference is that guns alone allow weaker victims to resist bigger, younger, stronger (and more often male) attackers. So laws aimed at depriving everyone of guns do not just fail to do any good. To the extent such laws take guns away from victims, that will actually increase violent crime by removing the one form of weapon that distinctively aids victims against criminals.

> "The bodies of young gunshot victims are streaming into urban hospital trauma centers on the front lines of an undeclared war on America's children."

Gun Violence Poses a Serious Threat to Children

Marian Wright Edelman

Too many American children are dying from gunshot wounds, argues Marian Wright Edelman in the following viewpoint. Indeed, she maintains, gunshot wounds are the second leading cause of death for American children, surpassed only by auto accidents. The United States has the morally alarming distinction of having the highest rate of child gun deaths of any developed nation, Edelman claims. Commonsense gun safety laws and conflict resolution alternatives can help make communities safe for children, she asserts. Edelman, a lawyer and children's rights advocate, is president and founder of the Children's Defense Fund.

As you read, consider the following questions:

1. According to the author, under what circumstances does a society know something is seriously wrong?

Marian Wright Edelman, "Protect Children, Not Guns," *Washington Informer*, vol. 42, June 22–28, 2006, pp. 24–25. Copyright © 2006 Washington Informer. Reproduced by permission.

2. What group of children is disproportionately affected by gun violence?

3. What, according to the author, can parents do to make their children safe from gun violence?

Is protecting our children important to us as a nation? On June 12 [2006], the Children's Defense Fund (CDF) released an annual report on gun violence against children, "Protect Children, Not Guns." The report shows that the number of children and teens who died from gun violence in 2003— 2,827—is higher than the number of American men and women killed in hostile action in Iraq from 2003 to April 2006. The bodies of young gunshot victims are streaming into urban hospital trauma centers on the front lines of an undeclared war on America's children.

Diverse Victims

The children who die every year from gunshot wounds come from all racial groups and are all ages. Some of them are too young to start kindergarten. In 2003, 56 preschoolers were killed by firearms while 52 law enforcement officers were killed in the line of duty. When it's more dangerous to be a preschooler than an on-duty police officer, we know something is seriously wrong in our society. The deaths of thousands of children each year are morally obscene for the world's most powerful nation, which has more resources to address social ills than any other nation.

The "Protect Children, Not Guns" report is being released as a number of U.S. mayors are demanding action from the White House and Congress to stop gun violence. In April, 15 mayors gathered for a summit on gun violence led by New York Mayor Michael Bloomberg and Boston Mayor Thomas Menino. I strongly applaud Mayor Bloomberg's statement that "It is time for national leadership in the war on gun violence."

But sadly, for tens of thousands of children and teens, long overdue leadership in the war on gun violence will come too late.

Deadly Facts

There are a few more deadly facts outlined in CDF's new report on the toll gun violence is taking on America's children. More 10- to 19-year-olds die from gunshot wounds than from any other cause except motor vehicle accidents. Almost 90 percent of the children and teens killed by firearms in 2003 were boys. Boys ages 15 to 19 are nearly nine times as likely as girls of the same age to be killed by firearms.

There were more than nine times as many suicides by guns among white children and teens as among black children and teens. But despite white youths' higher rate of gun suicides, gun violence still disproportionately affects black children. The firearm death rate for black males ages 15 to 19 is more than four times that of white males the same age. More black children and teens have been killed by firearms over the past six years than all the black people of all ages we lost in the history of lynchings.

Where is our voice? Why don't we care and protest when our children are being killed and killing others? It's time for us black adults to get our act together.

An Immoral Distinction

The seven states that recorded the most firearms deaths among children and teens in 2003 were California, Texas, Illinois, New York, Pennsylvania, Florida and North Carolina. The U.S. has the immoral distinction of having the highest rate of child firearm deaths. The rate of firearm deaths among children under age 15 is far higher in the U.S. than in 25 other industrialized countries combined.

Facts About Kids and Guns

- Every nine hours a child or teen was killed in a firearm-related accident or suicide in 2005.

- On average, 3 children died every day in non-homicide firearm incidents from 2000–2005.

- Since 1990, more than 5,000 children have been killed in firearm accidents.

- In *each* of the 10 years [since 1995], more than 1,000 kids committed suicide with a firearm; 105 were under 15 years old. *Centers for Disease Control and Prevention's National Center for Health Statistics, 1996–2005.*

Common Sense About Kids and Guns,
"Facts About Kids and Guns," 1999–2010.
www.kidsandguns.org.

"We have many more handguns and much weaker gun laws than any other country," said Harvard Professor David Hemenway, who has worked to develop strategies to combat illegal firearms.

What can we do to change this? CDF calls for the support of commonsense gun safety measures; congressional passage of legislation that closes the gun show loophole requiring criminal background checks on those purchasing guns from unlicensed dealers; and renewal of the ban on assault weapons.

Parents should remove guns from their homes; organize nonviolent conflict resolution support groups in their congregations and communities; monitor what their children watch on TV and listen in to our violence-hyped culture; and refuse to buy video games and other products for their children that glamorize violence or make it socially acceptable or fun.

Community leaders should turn schools and places of worship into venues of quality summer and after-school programs for children as positive alternatives to the streets and with positive role models. They should also adopt proven programs like Ceasefire Initiatives that bring families, faith groups, social service providers, and the police together to halt the killing of teens by other teens.

It's imperative that we work together to make our homes, our streets, and our communities safe from firearms now for the sake of our children.

"Fatal firearm accidents have been reduced more than two-thirds since the
inception of the [National Rifle Association of America's gun safety] program."

Gun Safety Programs Reduce
the Threat of Fatal Firearm
Accidents Among Children

National Rifle Association-Institute for Legislative Action

Programs such as the Eddie Eagle GunSafe Program reduce fatal
gun accidents among children, asserts the National Rifle
Association-Institute for Legislative Action (NRA-ILA) in the
following viewpoint. Eddie Eagle teaches children the distinction
between gun use in popular culture and in real life and how to
respond when they encounter an unsupervised gun, the NRA-
ILA maintains. Indeed, the program has been endorsed by many
youth and criminal justice organizations. NRA-ILA is an organization that lobbies for limited gun control legislation.

National Rifle Association-Institute for Legislative Action, "NRA Victories: Eighteen Million Safe Kids," *America's 1st Freedom*, July 2006. Copyright © 2006 National Rifle Association. Reproduced by permission.

As you read, consider the following questions:

1. How many children has the Eddie Eagle program reached?

2. What does Eddie Eagle suggest children do when they encounter an unsupervised gun?

3. How much money does it cost per year to maintain and deliver the Eddie Eagle program?

Shawna Dennet knew something was very wrong when her seven-year-old daughter Briana ran through their St. George, Utah, home screaming: "If you see a gun: Stop! Don't Touch! Leave the Area. Tell an Adult!"

Shawna raced to Briana, asking where she saw a gun—it was in a bedroom where a visiting relative was staying. There, Shawna found her four-year-old son holding a gun as her two younger children looked on.

When Paul and Kathryn Waiters of Gladstone, Mich., moved into a new house with their three children, they didn't know the previous owner had left a .22 bolt action rifle and a few rounds of ammunition in a closet corner where neither parent could fit.

Seven-year-old Michelle Waiters and twin four-year-old siblings Samantha and Christopher found the gun during a game of hide and seek. Michelle immediately commanded the younger children, "Stop! Don't Touch. Leave the Area. Tell an Adult."

A Groundbreaking Gun Accident Prevention Program

The Dennet and Waiters families—and countless others—credit the NRA's [National Rifle Association of America's] Eddie Eagle GunSafe Program for teaching their kids how to prevent a potentially fatal accident.

The Myth of the Child Gun Death Epidemic

More children will die in a car, drown in a pool, or choke on food than they will by firearms.... Children are at a 2,000 percent greater risk from the car in their driveway, than they are by the gun in their parents' closet. Children are almost 7 times more likely to drown than to be shot, and they are 130 percent more likely to die from choking on their dinner.

Gun Owners Foundation,
"Gun Control Fact-Sheet," March 2004.

This groundbreaking gun accident prevention program for children in pre-K through third grade has reached more than 18 million children in all 50 states, as well as Canada, Puerto Rico and beyond.

The Eddie Eagle GunSafe Program was the brainchild of NRA past president Marion P. Hammer in response to anti-gun propaganda disguised as "safety" curriculum flooding our nation's elementary schools.

The NRA worked with schoolteachers and administrators, clinical psychologists, law enforcement officers, education specialists and firearm experts to develop a message that's readily understood by children and easily taught by any adult:

"If you see a gun: Stop! Don't Touch. Leave the Area. Tell an Adult."

Praise for the Program

Over the years, the program has been praised by numerous groups and elected officials, including the Community Service and Youth Activities Divisions of the National Safety Council, the U.S. Department of Justice, the National Sheriffs' Association and 26 state governors, to name just a few.

Among children in the Eddie Eagle age group, fatal firearm accidents have been reduced more than two-thirds since the inception of the program, according to the National Center for Health Statistics.

What's more, a 2001 study published in the *Journal of Emergency Nursing Online* named Eddie Eagle the most effective among the more than 80 programs evaluated, drawing a distinct correlation between the Eddie Eagle Program and children's lives saved.

Statistics aside, it's the volume of testimonials that the NRA receives each year from parents that proves the true value of the Eddie Eagle Program.

Another recent example is the case of Billy Thornton, a third-grade student from Knoxville, Tenn. Billy found a security guard's loaded firearm in a credit union bathroom. He had recently learned the Eddie Eagle message, so he alerted his father to the presence of the unsupervised firearm. For this, Thornton received an award from his community.

Eddie Eagle has been honored and endorsed by various groups such as the U.S. Department of Justice, the Community Service and Youth Activities Divisions of the National Safety Council, the American Legion, the Police Athletic League, the National School Public Relations [Association], the National Association of School Safety and Law Enforcement Officers, as well as the National Sheriffs' Association (NSA).

In fact, when formally endorsing the Eddie Eagle GunSafe Program in March 2002, then NSA president Sheriff John Cary Bittick said, "We are proud to partner with the National Rifle Association on this very important issue, and we would like to express our full support for this program."

The Eddie Eagle GunSafe Program has also garnered praise from 49 state legislatures and/or governors, who have urged their respective state school systems to implement the life-saving message the program offers.

And the Community Service Division of the National Safety Council recognized the tremendous contribution that the Eddie Eagle Program has made in keeping kids safe by awarding program creator Marion P. Hammer with one of its highest honors, the Community Safety Award Citation for Outstanding Community Service.

Since 1996, the program's delivery has been enhanced by the availability of Eddie Eagle mascot costumes to law enforcement agencies that teach the program, helping capture children's attention during presentations.

Officer Rolando Hinjosa of the Melvindale, Mich., Police Department, said, "I can't say enough about the Eddie Eagle Program. It is going over great with teachers, administrators, parents and kids. The costume is an absolutely fantastic asset to teaching the program."

Keeping the Eddie Eagle GunSafe Program alive costs about $500,000 per year, on top of the millions NRA has invested in it from its inception through 2005. While funds raised through Friends of NRA and donations to the NRA Foundation help sustain the program, continued support is critical.

NRA membership is not required to teach the Eddie Eagle GunSafe Program, and the lessons can be adapted from one- to five-day formats. Materials include workbooks, an animated video, instructor guides, brochures and student-reward stickers, all of which are available in Spanish, too.

Answering the Critics

Anti-gun groups continue to be harsh critics of the program, apparently because it's preferred over their anti-gun "safety" curricula. But the Eddie Eagle GunSafe Program makes no judgment call as to whether guns are good or bad. And Eddie himself never touches a firearm.

In a recent example, an organization called PAX attempted to block efforts by District Attorney Edward Jagels to introduce Eddie Eagle to all kindergarten students in Kern County, Calif. PAX attacked the program in a letter to the school board, and anti-gun zealot Dr. Arthur Kellerman criticized it on Fox News. But Jagels and School Superintendent Larry Reider countered the criticism and put the safety of children over political gain. Today, all the district's principals have received Eddie Eagle program materials for use in their schools.

The NRA holds that all children—especially those who don't grow up around firearms—need to know what to do if they come upon an unsupervised gun. By drawing this distinction between guns on TV or in movies, and guns in real life, Eddie Eagle teaches children they should never touch a firearm without adult supervision.

As the program's creator Marion Hammer said, "The NRA is committed to helping keep America's children safe. This program also instills in our youth the important values of leadership, discipline and personal responsibility that will help our children throughout their lives." That's not indoctrination. That's an NRA commitment that can benefit every child.

Periodical Bibliography

The following articles have been selected to supplement the diverse views presented in this chapter.

Philip J. Cook, Wendy Cukier, and Keith Krause — "The Illicit Firearms Trade in North America," *Criminology & Criminal Justice*, vol. 9, no. 3, August 2009.

Marian Wright Edelman — "We Must Pay Attention to the Rise of Gun Violence," *Culvert Chronicles* (New York), July 3–9, 2008.

Dan Gifford and Michael I. Krauss — "Mexican Standoff on Second Amendment," *Investor's Business Daily*, July 8, 2009.

Barry Glassner — "Still Fearful After All These Years," *Chronicle of Higher Education*, January 17, 2010.

Kenneth Jost — "Gun Violence," *CQ Researcher*, May 5, 2007.

James N. Logue — "Violent Death in American Schools in the 21st Century: Reflections Following the 2006 Amish School Shootings," *Journal of School Health*, January 2008.

Megan McArdle — "Gun Statistics," *Atlantic*, June 26, 2008.

New York Times — "Loopholes and More Loopholes," May 2, 2007.

Rebecca Peters — "Small Arms: No Single Solution," *UN Chronicle*, 2009.

Rob Walker — "Crossfire," *New York Times Magazine*, March 22, 2010.

OPPOSING
VIEWPOINTS®
SERIES

CHAPTER 2

What Factors Contribute
to Gun Violence?

Chapter Preface

A lmost immediately following the tragic shooting deaths of thirty-two students and teachers at Virginia Tech on April 16, 2007, commentators began to debate what led the killer to such a horrific act. The public soon learned that Korean-born Seung-Hui Cho had exhibited bizarre and aggressive behavior that had troubled Cho's parents, peers, and teachers. In fact, in December 2005, after Cho threatened suicide, Virginia judge Paul Barnett ordered Cho to receive outpatient psychiatric treatment, having found Cho to be "an imminent danger to himself."[1] The Gun Control Act of 1968 prohibits possession of a firearm by anyone "adjudicated as a mental defective."[2] The federal law defines a "mental defective" as a person who "is a danger to himself or others."[3] The regulations broadly define adjudication to include "a determination by a court, board, commission or other lawful authority."[4] Thus, federal law would have disqualified Cho from buying a handgun.

Nevertheless, in the early months of 2007, Cho purchased a .22-caliber Walther P22, a 9mm Glock, and fifty rounds of ammunition. Cho presented his Virginia driver's license, his checkbook, and his immigration card—identification suffi-cient to complete the required federal background check for handgun purchases. The database said to proceed with the sale. Virginia authorities did not put Judge Barnett's order into the federal background-check system because Virginia law requires commitment to a mental hospital to prevent an applicant from buying a gun. Thus, gun dealers had no reason to block Cho's purchases. Claiming this gap in the background-check system played a significant role in the Virginia Tech

1. Brigid Schulte and Chris L. Jenkins, "Cho Didn't Get Court-Ordered Treatment," *Washington Post*, May 7, 2007.
2. 18 U.S.C. § 922(d)(4).
3. Ibid.
4. 27 CFR 555.11.

shooting, some analysts immediately began to call for laws to plug gaps between state and federal laws. While few dispute that mental illness can, in some cases, lead to gun violence, commentators do debate whether the connection between mental illness and gun violence is significant enough to enact such laws.

Supporters claim that gaps in the system made Cho's killing spree possible. Paul Helmke, president of the Brady Campaign to Prevent Gun Violence, argues that Cho was able to buy the weapons because of what he calls "lethal loopholes" in the background-check system. A May 2007 report of the pro–gun control group the Third Way reveals that only twenty-two states put mental records into the system, "rendering . . . the [federal] law useless in most states."[5] A proposed bill would strengthen the rules and help fund state participation in the National Instant Criminal Background Check System (NICS). The National Rifle Association of America (NRA), an organization that generally opposes most limits on the right of American citizens to own guns, supports the legislation. "We've been on record for decades that records of those adjudicated as mentally defective and deemed to be a danger to others or to themselves should be part of the national instant-check system and not be allowed to own a firearm,"[6] states NRA representative Andrew Arulanandam. "The mental health lobby and the medical lobby are the impediments—they are against release of records,"[7] Arulanandam maintains.

Mental health groups do in fact caution against overly broad labels that identify mental illness as an indicator of potential violence. "It's very easy and very tempting when something as horrible as Virginia Tech occurs to assume that mental illness correlates with a propensity for violence,"[8] argues

5. Third Way, "Missing Records: Holes in Background Check System Allow Illegal Buyers to Get Guns," May 14, 2007.
6. Quoted in Kenneth Jost, "Gun Violence," *CQ Researcher*, May 25, 2007.
7. Ibid.
8. Quoted in Kenneth Jost, "Gun Violence," *CQ Researcher*, May 25, 2007.

Ron Honberg, director of policy and legal affairs for the National Alliance on Mental Illness. According to Honberg, however, "that's not borne out for the majority of people with mental illness." Many of those who may once have been mentally disabled "have gone on to recover and are living independently and are working and are upstanding citizens." Widespread reporting, opponents argue, could lead to discrimination that might deter people from seeking treatment. "We have real grave concerns about people with mental illness being a population that's singled out," Honberg claims.

Whether the connection between mental illness and gun violence is significant enough to warrant laws to strengthen the federal background-check system remains hotly contested. The authors of the viewpoints in the following chapter debate what other factors contribute to gun violence.

| *"This is an insanely violent society, and the worst of that violence is made insanely easy by the widespread availability of guns."* |

The Availability of Guns Increases Gun Violence

Bob Herbert

Of the thousands of people murdered each year, most are shot, a tragedy made easy by the prevalence of guns in the United States, claims Bob Herbert in the following viewpoint. Finding a weapon is easy for murderers because gun regulations are so lax, he asserts. Despite the enormous cost of gun violence, Americans lack the political will to do anything about it, Herbert argues. Indeed, he reasons, gun violence is so common in the United States that the outrage necessary to pass laws that will reduce the problem is difficult to maintain. Herbert comments on politics, urban affairs, and social trends for the New York Times.

As you read, consider the following questions:

1. Why, according to the author, is it hard for individual cases of gun violence to remain in the public mind?

2. In addition to murder, in what other ways are people killed by guns?

3. According to the Brady Campaign, how many children and teenagers are shot but survive in a typical year?

Philip Markoff, a medical student, supposedly carried his semiautomatic in a hollowed-out volume of *Gray's Anatomy*. Police believe he used it in a hotel room in Boston last week [April 2009] to murder Julissa Brisman, a 26-year-old woman who had advertised her services as a masseuse on Craigslist.

In Palm Harbor, Fla., a 12-year-old boy named Jacob Larson came across a gun in the family home that, according to police, his parents had forgotten they had. Jacob shot himself in the head and is in a coma, police said. Authorities believe the shooting was accidental.

Violence Made Easy

There is no way to overstate the horror of gun violence in America. Roughly 16,000 to 17,000 Americans are murdered every year, and more than 12,000 of them, on average, are shot to death. This is an insanely violent society, and the worst of that violence is made insanely easy by the widespread availability of guns.

When the music producer Phil Spector decided, for whatever reason, to kill the actress, Lana Clarkson, all he had to do was reach for his gun—one of the 283 million privately owned firearms that are out there. When [sniper] John Muhammad and his teenage accomplice, Lee Malvo, went on a killing spree that took 10 lives in the Washington [D.C.] area, the absolute least of their worries was how to get a semiautomatic rifle that fit their deadly mission.

We're confiscating shampoo from carry-on luggage at airports while at the same time handing out high-powered weaponry to criminals and psychotics at gun shows.

The United States Has Millions of Guns in Civilian Hands

- The U.S. has an estimated 283 million guns in civilian hands or approximately 97 guns for every 100 people.

- Each year, about 4.5 million new firearms, including approximately 2 million handguns, are sold in the United States.

- An estimated 2 million secondhand firearms are sold each year.

- In 2007, police recovered at least 232,308 guns in connection with crime.

- Gun owners throw away an estimated 36,000 guns every year.

Brady Campaign to Prevent Gun Violence,
"Guns in America: Overview," 2009. www.bradycampaign.org.

There were ceremonies marking the recent 10th anniversary of the shootings at Columbine High School, but very few people remember a mass murder just five months after Columbine, when a man with a semiautomatic handgun opened fire on congregants praying in a Baptist church in Fort Worth. Eight people died, including the gunman, who shot himself.

A little more than a year before the Columbine killings, two boys with high-powered rifles killed a teacher and four little girls at a school in Jonesboro, Ark. That's not widely remembered either. When something is as pervasive as gun violence in the U.S., which is as common as baseball in the summertime, it's very hard for individual cases to remain in the public mind.

Homicides are only a part of the story.

The Toil of Gun Violence

While more than 12,000 people are murdered with guns annually, the Brady Campaign to Prevent Gun Violence (using the latest available data) tells us that more than 30,000 people are killed over the course of one typical year by guns. That includes 17,000 who commit suicide, nearly 800 who are killed in accidental shootings and more than 300 killed by the police. (In many of the law enforcement shootings, the police officers are reacting to people armed with guns.)

And then there are the people who are shot but don't die. Nearly 70,000 fall into that category in a typical year, including 48,000 who are criminally attacked, 4,200 who survive a suicide attempt, more than 15,000 who are shot accidentally, and more than 1,000—many with a gun in possession—who are shot by the police.

The medical cost of treating gunshot wounds in the U.S. is estimated to be well more than $2 billion annually. And the Violence Policy Center, a gun control advocacy group, has noted that nonfatal gunshot wounds are the leading cause of uninsured hospital stays.

The toll on children and teenagers is particularly heartbreaking. According to the Brady Campaign, more than 3,000 kids are shot to death in a typical year. More than 1,900 are murdered, more than 800 commit suicide, about 170 are killed accidentally and 20 or so are killed by the police.

Another 17,000 are shot but survive.

A Blasé Attitude

I remember writing from Chicago two years ago about the nearly three dozen public school youngsters who were shot to death in a variety of circumstances around the city over the course of just one school year. Arne Duncan, who was then the chief of the Chicago schools and is now the U.S. secretary of education, said to me at the time: "That's more than a kid every two weeks. Think about that."

Actually, that's our problem. We don't really think about it. If the crime is horrible enough, we'll go through the motions of public anguish but we never really do anything about it. Americans are as blasé as can be about this relentless slaughter that keeps the culture soaked in blood.

This blasé attitude, this willful refusal to acknowledge the scope of the horror, leaves the gun nuts free to press their crazy case for more and more guns in ever more hands. They're committed to keeping the killing easy, and we should be committed for not stopping them.

> "*Everyone wants to take guns from criminals, but banning guns ends up meaning only criminals, not law-abiding citizens, have them.*" ⟨1⟩

Making Guns Less Available Does Not Reduce Gun Violence

John R. Lott Jr.

Policies that limit a law-abiding citizen's access to guns do not reduce gun violence, argues John R. Lott Jr. in the following viewpoint. In fact, he maintains, gun bans have done little to reduce crime in the cities that have banned them. For example, Lott asserts, the murder rate in Washington, D.C., began to fall before the city's gun ban and rose after it went into effect. Gun bans do not prevent criminals from obtaining guns, he reasons; bans simply ensure that only criminals have guns. Lott is author of The Bias Against Guns: Why Almost Everything You've Heard About Gun Control Is Wrong *and* More Guns, Less Crime: Understanding Crime and Gun Control Laws.

As you read, consider the following questions:

1. How did the murder rate in Washington, D.C., compare to the U.S. rate as a whole after its handgun ban went into effect?

2. What does the author argue was the impact of Chicago's handgun ban?

3. What, according to the author, has become the ultimate scapegoat for politicians' failure to control crime?

Banning handguns is all the rage. [Toronto, Ontario] Mayor David Miller's push for a national ban has been joined by other Canadian big-city mayors. Yet, dissatisfied with progress at the national level, Miller successfully asked city council this week to approve measures to further discourage gun ownership in Toronto, such as shutting down city-owned gun ranges.

Gun Bans and Murder Rates

While it may seem obvious to many people that banning handguns will save lives and cut crime, the experience in the United States suggests differently. Two major U.S. cities— Washington, D.C., and Chicago—have tried banning handguns. . . .

Washington's ban went into effect in early 1977, but since it started there has been only one year (1985) when its murder rate fell below what it was in 1976. Murder rates were falling before the ban and rose afterward. In the five years before the ban, the murder rate fell from 37 to 27 murders per 100,000 people. In the five years after it went into effect, the rate rose back up to 35.

D.C.'s murder rate also rose dramatically relative to other cities. In the 29 years that we have data after the ban, D.C.'s murder rate ranked first or second among the largest 50 U.S. cities for 15 years. In another four years, it ranked fourth. By contrast, in 1976, its murder rate ranked 15th.

Gun Crimes Capture Public Attention

Statistics suggest that any gun control measures are unlikely to make any serious dents in crime. . . .

Gun crimes, however, capture the attention of the public in ways other attacks do not. In Vancouver [British Columbia] in late May [2007], for instance, 13-year-old Chris Poeun was stabbed to death in a brawl with other youngsters outside a science museum. The case attracted little attention, but the May 23 shooting of 15-year-old Jordan Manners at his high school, C.W. Jefferys Collegiate Institute in Toronto, filled headlines across the country.

Jordan Michael Smith, "Crimes and Misconceptions,"
Western Standard (Vancouver), July 30, 2007.

Not only did Washington's murder rate rise much faster than other cities, it rose more quickly than neighbouring Maryland's and Virginia's or the U.S. rate as a whole.

Similarly for overall violent crime, there have only been two years after the ban when D.C.'s violent crime rate fell below the rate in 1976.

Surely D.C. has had many problems that contribute to crime, but even cities with far better police departments have seen murder and violent crime soar in the wake of handgun bans. Chicago has banned all handguns since 1982. But that handgun ban didn't work at all when it came to reducing violence. Chicago's murder rate fell from 27 to 22 per 100,000 in the five years before the law and then rose slightly to 23. Chicago's murder rate rose relative to other large cities and its five neighbouring Illinois counties.

Where Gun Bans Increase Violent Crime

But the experience in other countries, even island nations that have gone so far as banning handguns and where borders are easy to monitor, should give Mr. Miller and his supporters some pause. These are places that just can't blame the United States or other neighbouring states for the failure of their gun-control laws. Not only didn't violent crime and homicide decline as promised, but they actually increased.

Great Britain banned handguns in January 1997. But the number of deaths and injuries from gun crime in England and Wales increased 340% in the seven years from 1998 to 2005. The rates of serious violent crime, armed robberies, rapes and homicide have also soared. The Republic of Ireland and Jamaica also experienced large increases in murder rates after enacting handgun bans.

Everyone wants to take guns from criminals, but banning guns ends up meaning only criminals, not law-abiding citizens, have them. Just as it is extremely hard to stop illegal drugs from getting into Canada, drug gangs seem to find ways to bring in the guns. The weapons the Canadian border guards seize at the U.S. border are overwhelmingly from unwitting U.S. tourists. Few criminals smuggling guns are caught.

Possibly Toronto and Canada will somehow operate differently from the rest of the world, but gun control has become the ultimate scapegoat for politicians' failure to control crime. One hopes politicians will learn it is the law-abiding citizens, not criminals, who obey the bans.

| "NRA policies handcuff national law enforcement's ability to effectively regulate private gun sales, gun shows, and even the sharing of crime-gun trace data."

Pro-Gun Organization Policies Promote Gun Violence

John E. Rosenthal

Despite public support for gun control legislation, pro-gun organizations continue to block such legislation, maintains John E. Rosenthal in the following viewpoint. Gun manufacturers invest heavily in the National Rifle Association of America (NRA), which in turn spends millions to oppose commonsense gun laws, he claims. In fact, Rosenthal argues, the NRA opposes background checks for people on the terrorist watch list. As a result, he reasons, these organizations make it difficult for law enforcement to regulate gun sales and thus put guns into the hands of terrorists, criminals, and the mentally ill. Rosenthal, a gun owner, is also a gun control activist and cofounder of Stop Handgun Violence.

John E. Rosenthal, "Had Enough Gun Violence?" *Christian Science Monitor*, February 20, 2008. Reproduced by permission of the author.

As you read, consider the following questions:

1. What rights does Rosenthal claim should not be extended to terrorists, criminals, and children?

2. How can one obtain an armor-piercing sniper rifle?

3. According to the Federal Election Commission, how much has the NRA spent on congressional candidates?

Let's get this out of the way. I am a gun owner and a staunch supporter of the Second Amendment. What I do not support is extending the rights embedded in the Second Amendment to terrorists, criminals, and children.

In the wake of a horrific campus shooting at Northern Illinois University, where 21 students were shot, we're reminded *again* that national gun laws must be strengthened.

The Weakening of Gun Laws

Sadly, gun laws have only been weakened since the massacres at Columbine High School and Virginia Tech.[1] To be sure, these headline-grabbing mass shootings may not have been preventable. But beyond the headlines, consider this news: 83 Americans die *each and every* day from gun violence. And much of that violence is very preventable.

Current federal law allows an unlimited number of easily concealable handguns and military-style weapons to be sold privately in 32 states without a criminal background check or an ID. Why do we take such a hands-off approach to these dangerous weapons? The National Rifle Association [of America] (NRA) and the gun industry lobby are a big part of the answer.

You have to show ID to purchase alcohol or cigarettes. But if you want a Barrett .50-caliber sniper rifle (capable of pen-

1. On April 20, 1999, Eric Harris and Dylan Klebold killed twelve students and one teacher at Columbine High School before killing themselves. On April 16, 2007, student Seung-Hui Cho killed thirty-two people and wounded many others at Virginia Tech University before killing himself.

etrating steel and taking out an armored vehicle from more than a mile) you need only to show up at one of 5,000 legal gun shows and fork over the cash—no ID or background check required! It is well documented that al Qaeda, Hezbollah, and IRA [Irish Republican Army] terrorists have exploited this loophole in US gun laws to purchase military-style weapons from "private sellers" at gun shows.

In a recent radio debate with me, an NRA official confirmed that the organization is opposed to uniform criminal background checks for fear they will "shut down gun shows." The NRA says that not even people on the suspected terrorist watch list should be barred from purchasing guns because—are you ready for this?—"we do not know how people are put on the list" and "many times people are victims of mistaken identity."

Blocking Commonsense Laws

Eighty-nine percent of Americans said they wanted mandatory background checks for anyone buying a gun, according to a 2007 Greenberg Quinlan Rosner Research and the Tarrance Group survey. But the NRA has continually blocked such commonsense legislation as mandatory background checks and five-day waiting periods to buy a handgun. NRA policies handcuff national law enforcement's ability to effectively regulate private gun sales, gun shows, and even the sharing of crime-gun trace data within the law enforcement community.

By putting guns into the hands of terrorists, criminals, and the mentally ill, the policies the NRA helped create a society where defense by guns becomes mandatory. Meanwhile, the bank accounts of the NRA leaders and lobbyists are enriched and congressional coffers are replenished. Gun manufacturers reinforce this cycle by investing in the NRA.

According to Federal Election Commission reports the NRA has spent more than $22 million on congressional candidates in order to support its agenda during the past four election cycles. In 2004, the NRA spent nearly $4 million to reelect George W. Bush.

Immunity from lawsuits and freedom from consumer protection regulations and manufacturing standards are just a few of the benefits delivered by the NRA and provided by a complicit president and Congress.

Evidence of Gun-Law Success

Massachusetts stands out as an example of a state that has successful gun violence prevention legislation. Along with 17 other states, it has enacted background checks for all gun sales. Only Hawaii has a firearms fatality rate lower than that of Massachusetts. Hawaii is fortunate; bordered by water, it is less accessible to gun traffickers than Massachusetts, where more than 60 percent of guns traced to crime come from out of state. Bay State neighbors New Hampshire, Vermont, and Maine are three of the top four crime-gun source states for Massachusetts, where guns are easily purchased by prohibited buyers without a background check or an ID.

Most law-abiding citizens like me buy guns from federally licensed dealers required to perform background checks. Incredibly, federal law allows criminals and terrorists who can't pass background checks to easily buy guns from private individuals in 32 states without detection.

The bloodshed in our communities and schools (there were multiple campus shootings last week [February 2008]!) is largely preventable. Of course, not every law is going to stop violence completely, but shouldn't we help prevent the tragedies we can by weeding out the criminals? It is time for reasonable people—the majority of Americans who agree with me—to insist that Congress enact sensible and consistent federal laws that require criminal background checks for *all* gun sales in the US.

> *"[Gun violence is] the result of too many dysfunctional households, failing schools, drug and alcohol abuse and a saturation of music that promotes self-destruction."*

Gun Violence Is a Symptom of Other Social Problems

Courtland Milloy

Asking gun manufacturers and gun stores to end gun violence is fruitless, claims Courtland Milloy in the following viewpoint. Gun violence is a symptom of other social problems, he argues. Moreover, Milloy maintains, in communities that suffer disproportionately from gun violence, the culture often promotes self-destruction. When young people causing problems in these communities carry guns, responsible adults are discouraged from intervening, he asserts. Milloy is a columnist for the Washington Post.

As you read, consider the following questions:

1. What did African American men checking out large-caliber firearms at Realco Guns tell Milloy was the reason they wanted a gun?

2. What did those who wanted to force Realco Guns out of business believe would be accomplished?

3. What does the author claim largely rural, conservative whites are protecting and why?

Not long ago, I brought my gun to Realco Guns in District Heights [Maryland] for cleaning. It is a vintage, J.C. Higgins .22-caliber rifle that my dad purchased from Sears around 1964. We belonged to a father-and-son club in my hometown, Shreveport, La., and this was the gun we used whenever the group went out to shoot at tin cans.

In the middle of so much gun violence, it's not easy to cling to fond memories of those days.

During my visit to Realco, several young African American men were checking out large-caliber firearms in a display case. I asked some of them why they wanted a gun.

"Protection," one replied.

"You never know who you might run into," another said.

Nobody mentioned shooting tin cans with Dad.

Protesting Gun Violence

A protest rally was held outside the gun store yesterday [August 2007]. It turns out that Realco, according to federal data, is the Washington [D.C.] region's biggest source of firearms used in crimes. Apparently guns purchased legally from the store have been resold to or stolen by people who aren't supposed to have them. So several dozen protesters gathered to chant: "Stop the violence! Save the children!" Some even believed that forcing Realco out of business would help to accomplish those things.

"Since I became mayor, getting rid of guns and closing down this store have been high on my list of priorities," District Heights Mayor James Walls told me at the rally. "They've

Gun Homicide by Race/Ethnicity: Rank of Gun Homicide Rate, Rates of Gun Homicide, and Number of Gun Homicides, 2006

Rank	Race/Ethnicity	Gun Homicide Death Rate per 100,000 People	Number of Gun Homicides
1	Black	18.62	7,021
2	Hispanic	5.61	2,472
3	American Indian-Alaska Native	4.39	109
4	Asian/Pacific Islander	1.95	270
5	White	1.43	2,860

TAKEN FROM: Brady Center to Prevent Gun Violence, 2009. http://www.bradycampaign.org/facts/gunviolence/factsethnicity.

got to come to us for business permits, and we'll be taking a close look at their role in the gun violence that is killing so many of our people."

Realco declined to comment, but an employee released a statement declaring that all its firearms sales are legal and follow procedures set by the FBI [Federal Bureau of Investigation] and the Maryland State Police.

The protest was organized by the Rainbow/PUSH Coalition, founded by the Rev. Jesse Jackson. Not far away, gun advocates staged a counterprotest to decry the dropping of murder charges in cases in which witnesses were too afraid to testify.

"Stop [expletive] and start snitching," one yelled into a loudspeaker.

Not the best way to make a case for gun rights. But the gun control folks have their shortcomings, too.

Someone read a statement from Jackson urging "gun shops and gun manufacturers to stop the epidemic of rising gun violence."

The Cultural Connection

Excuse me, but I just don't see why any black person would expect gun manufacturers and dealers to help us stop killing ourselves. At Realco, guys pull into the parking lot in big SUVs [sport-utility vehicles] with tinted glass and spinning rims. They look like gangbangers from a rap music video. If some gun control advocates had their way, Realco would reject those young black men as customers because they fit a racial profile. And Realco would be sued for not selling guns as surely as it was denounced yesterday for selling them.

And go to any major gun show—into the heart of America's white gun culture—and you'll find plenty of Confederate flags and supremacist literature on display. And even if everybody at the show doesn't subscribe to those views, the people there aren't offended enough to stay away.

This fight is not so much over guns as culture. Largely rural, conservative whites are protecting a gun-loving lifestyle because they care more about it than they care about the loss of black lives to gun violence in urban areas. And if you want to fight that culture, you have to have a culture to fight with.

"In my honest opinion, I'm not so concerned about the prevalence of guns," said Kenny Barnes, founder of a D.C.-based anti-gun violence campaign called Guns Aside. "Violence isn't the issue; it's a symptom. It's the result of too many dysfunctional households, failing schools, drug and alcohol abuse and a saturation of music that promotes self-destruction."

Guns Make Change Difficult

Daniel Webster, co-director of the Center for Gun Policy and Research at Johns Hopkins University, argues that rebuilding a culture, strengthening communities and families, is much harder when guns are in the mix.

"It used to be the case that adults in the community would not feel restrained if they saw teenagers getting into trouble, doing things that they shouldn't," he told me during a recent interview. "Now that doesn't occur because people are afraid that the youngsters are carrying guns. Guns have taken away what for centuries has been an effective means of social control. You can ask for greater involvement by concerned citizens, mentors, parents and teachers, but that becomes very difficult to do when the person causing the trouble has a gun."

Unless, perhaps, you have one, too.

The rifle that my dad bought in '64 was probably as much for home defense as for target practice. But protection is not why I wanted the gun. Realco made it look like new, and I plan to mount it as a showpiece, a reminder of the days when kids shot tin cans instead of one another.

| *"Guns and hate have been a toxic mix in this country for decades, and all signs suggest the combination is getting more dangerous."*

Hate and Extremist Groups Encourage Gun Violence

Astrid Dorélien, Michael Miller, and Peter Brody

The prevalence of hate groups combined with weak gun laws promote gun violence in the United States, argues Astrid Dorélien, Michael Miller, and Peter Brody in the following viewpoint. For example, the authors assert, white supremacist Benjamin Smith, while not legally permitted to buy guns, accumulated an arsenal of more than seventy guns and went on to kill two and wound nine people. The gun lobby fuels this toxic mix of guns and hate by wrongly suggesting that the government wants to take away Americans' guns. Dorélien, Miller, and Brody are interns at the Brady Center to Prevent Gun Violence.

As you read, consider the following questions:

1. From what ethnic and religious groups were the victims of Benjamin Smith's 1999 shooting spree?

Astrid Dorélien, Michael Miller, and Peter Brody, *Guns and Hate: A Lethal Combination.* Washington, DC: The Brady Center to Prevent Gun Violence, 2009. Copyright © 2009 Brady Center to Prevent Gun Violence. Reproduced by permission.

2. On what grounds did Scott Roeder justify his intention to kill Dr. George Tiller in 2009?

3. According to Richard Poplawski's mother, why did her son begin to stockpile guns?

On June 10, 2009, a white supremacist who believed it was "time to kill the Jews" took his gun to the Holocaust museum in Washington, D.C., and started shooting immediately upon entering, leaving a security guard dead. Ten years earlier, a white supremacist gunman terrorized the Midwest, shooting African Americans, Asians, and Jews throughout Illinois and Indiana, killing former Northwestern University basketball coach Ricky Byrdsong in Skokie, Illinois, and Indiana University graduate student Won-Joon Yoon in Bloomington, Indiana, and wounding nine more. In another hate-crime spree in 1999, five people were shot at a Los Angeles Jewish Community Center before the shooter shot and killed a U.S. postal worker. Other recent extremist shootings have targeted churchgoers, abortion providers, U.S. soldiers, and police officers.

The Gun-Hate Connection

These shootings created media shockwaves worldwide, but they should not have been surprising to those familiar with the prevalence of hate groups in America and our loophole-ridden gun laws that make it far too easy for dangerous people to obtain guns. Guns and hate have been a toxic mix in this country for decades, and all signs suggest the combination is getting more dangerous. Over 900 hate groups currently operate in the country, up from 602 in 2000. A recent report (since withdrawn) by the Department of Homeland Security found that "the consequences of a prolonged economic downturn," as well as "the election of the first African American president," could "create a fertile recruiting environment for right-wing extremism and even result in confrontations between such groups and government authorities."

At the same time, political leaders in Washington have failed to enact the laws needed to protect Americans from gun-wielding extremists. Benjamin Smith, the white supremacist who terrorized Illinois and Indiana a decade ago, was not legally permitted to buy guns because he was the subject of an active domestic violence restraining order, but was able to obtain his guns by exploiting gaping loopholes in our gun laws. These loopholes enabled a gun trafficker to acquire over 70 cheap handguns from a corrupt gun dealer, and enabled the killer to buy two of those guns without a background check, no questions asked. Ten years later, those loopholes remain, making it just as easy for dangerous people to obtain the means to realize their hate-filled visions. Gun shows continue to attract members of hate groups, who buy and sell neo-Nazi and extremist literature and paraphernalia, and, because of the gun show loophole, can buy and sell guns, no questions asked, with no background checks and no record of sale required. It is past time for our leaders in Washington to do what is needed to protect Americans, instead of cowering to the gun lobby.

Fueling the Hate

Adding fuel to this toxic mix is the incendiary rhetoric of the gun lobby. The National Rifle Association [of America, or NRA] continues to gin up fears of gun owners with false claims that President [Barack] Obama is intent on taking away their guns. While the gun lobby does not outwardly advocate violence, it should appreciate that its rhetoric can have far-reaching implications. It is disturbing, for example, that both the Holocaust museum killer and the crazed man who used an assault weapon to murder three Pittsburgh police officers absorbed and expressed the gun lobby's message that the government may be after their guns. Especially after the Supreme Court has held that the Second Amendment protects the right of law-abiding citizens to own guns in the home for self-defense, the gun lobby should rein in its rhetoric, and speak more truthfully and responsibly.

This report covers a decade of hate-motivated gun crimes, from the Benjamin Smith shootings of July 1999 to the June 2009 Holocaust museum shooting. The report is not intended as a comprehensive account of all hate crimes or shootings involving members of hate groups. Rather, through several prominent examples, it shows how loopholes in existing gun laws helped to enable the shooters and how inflammatory gun lobby rhetoric may have contributed to their violent outbursts.

A Neo-Nazi Shooting Spree

Benjamin Smith grew up in the suburbs of Chicago and emerged as a white supremacist while in college, where he passed out racist flyers and pamphlets. Smith attended both the University of Illinois and Indiana University. While at Indiana University, Smith's white supremacist activities led to his arrest by Bloomington, Indiana, police. Bloomington Police Chief Jim Kennedy called Smith a "right-wing extremist," though there was nothing Kennedy could legally do to prevent Smith's distribution of hate speech. According to Indiana University Dean of Students Richard McKaig, "There's no question you would call him a supremacist."

After leaving school, Smith moved to Morton, Illinois, near the East Peoria home base of Matthew Hale. Hale's white supremacist right-wing hate group, "World Church of the Creator," advocates "white superiority over 'mud people' of other ethnic backgrounds." Hale described Smith as "a pleasant person who believes in his people, the white people." Hale was arrested in 2003 for soliciting the murder of a judge and is now serving a 40-year sentence for the crime.

How Smith Got His Guns

Though Benjamin Smith was prohibited by law from obtaining firearms because of an active domestic violence restraining order against him, loopholes in the law enabled him to acquire his arsenal. He first went to a federally licensed firearms dealer, but was turned away after a Brady [Brady Handgun Violence Prevention Act] background check discovered the restraining order, which had been obtained by a former girlfriend. However, Smith was then able to find his guns in the classified advertisements of the Peoria *Journal Star*. In them, he found a listing placed by a gun trafficker named Donald Fiessinger.

On June 26, 1999, Smith, who had a shaved head and the phrase "Sabbath Breaker" tattooed on his chest, met up with Fiessinger, who sold Smith a handgun. Three days later, on June 29, Smith arranged to meet Fiessinger again, and purchased another handgun. These two guns were a Phoenix .22 and a Bryco .380, both "Saturday Night Specials," cheap, easily concealable handguns popular with criminals. Days later, federal agents raided Fiessinger's home, and he was arrested for illegal gun trafficking. Fiessinger was able to maintain his illegal gun business by continually buying guns from a reckless licensed firearms dealer, Old Prairie Trading Post.

After the shootings, law enforcement officers affirmed that Old Prairie must have known, under these circumstances, that Fiessinger was illegally reselling the guns. Indeed, Old Prairie admitted that it suspected exactly that and could have stopped selling guns to Fiessinger at any time, but instead chose to take his money and supply him with all the guns he could pay for. Thus, Fiessinger was able to amass and sell a small arsenal, and to supply illegal purchasers without background checks.

Fiessinger bought 72 cheap, low-quality handguns ("Saturday Night Specials") over less than two years from Old Prairie Trading Post, a federally licensed firearms dealer in Pekin, Illinois. No federal or state law prevented Fiessinger from amassing this inventory, as there are no limits on the number of handguns an individual is allowed to buy. Federal law only requires that when more than one handgun is purchased from a dealer in five business days, that the dealer send a multiple sale reporting form to the Bureau of Alcohol, Tobacco, Firearms and Explosives (ATF). However, the ATF has no authority to stop bulk firearms sales, and because Fiessinger's sales were staggered with gaps of one week or more, the law did not require this nominal reporting. As Old Prairie's owner, Robert Hayes, said of his sale of 72 handguns to Fiessinger, "Everything I did was fine, according to ATF guidelines." . . .

The Shootings

While living in Morton, Illinois, Smith had decided that it was time to launch "a one-man race war." Armed with the two guns he purchased from Fiessinger, Smith took his 1994 Ford Taurus and started his killing spree on the Friday before the Fourth of July in northern Chicago and its suburbs.

First, in Rogers Park, a Chicago neighborhood, Smith shot and wounded six Orthodox Jews on their way home from temple. Then, minutes later, in the nearby town of Skokie, Illinois, Smith shot and killed Ricky Byrdsong as he walked with two of his children near their home. The next day, Smith shot one man in Springfield, Illinois, then drove to Decatur, Illinois, and shot Reverend Stephen Anderson as he walked to a family July 4th weekend gathering. Then Smith drove to Urbana, Illinois, where he wounded an Asian American student at the University of Illinois, Stephen Kuo. Finally, on the third day of his rampage, Smith went to his old college town of Bloomington, Indiana, and killed Indiana University graduate student Won-Joon Yoon as he walked to church services. The string of shootings ended only after police chased him down near Salem, Illinois, and—just as they were about to make an arrest—Smith "shot himself below the chin." He died en route to the hospital.

In total, Smith wounded nine people and killed two, Won-Joon Yoon and Ricky Byrdsong, whose stories are told below. All eleven of Smith's victims were either Jewish, African American, or of Asian decent—all deemed "mud people" in the disturbed, racist ideology of the "World Church of the Creator," of which Smith was a member.

Benjamin Smith's Victims

The first man Smith killed was Ricky Byrdsong, a former Northwestern University basketball coach. Byrdsong had coached the Wildcats between 1993 and 1998, and took the perennial Big Ten doormat to the NIT [National Invitation Tournament] basketball tournament. Before that, he coached at the University of Detroit Mercy and was an assistant under Lute Olson at the University of Arizona. Byrdsong had been a basketball star in his own right before that, playing at Iowa State University.

After his time at Northwestern, Byrdsong decided to stay in the Chicago area and took a job at Aon Corp., an insurance company headquartered in Chicago. Byrdsong served as a vice president of the company, and according to Aon chairman Pat Ryan, "His leadership and inspirational skills led hundreds of Aon Corp. people to get involved in community work." Byrdsong, who served the First Presbyterian Church of Evanston, Illinois, as a deacon, had also written a book entitled *Coaching Your Kids in the Game of Life*. The book was released the Father's Day following his death.

At the time of his death, Byrdsong was out on a run with two of his children, Kelley, 10 and Ricky Jr., 8. The beautiful summer afternoon was punctuated by gunfire from a blue Ford Taurus, an unusual sound in the idyllic suburb of Skokie. Byrdsong was slain in front of his two children, though neither of them [was] shot. As Ricky Jr. recalled, "We saw this car coming, and we heard a bunch of shots." As Kelly remembers, "They sounded like fireworks. I saw a blue car turn. The shots were getting closer, and it was a lot louder. Then I saw a window cracked, and a gun was pointed out the window. And he just sprayed bullets past us." Ricky Jr., recollects, "I looked over and my dad was on the ground." In response to Byrdsong's death, his widow, Sherialyn, wrote, "The violent act that took my husband's life is yet another clarion call to our nation. It's time to wake up, America." Byrdsong is memorialized by the annual "Race Against Hate" that is held every summer in Evanston, Illinois. Sherialyn continues to speak out against hate and for stronger gun laws.

Later in Smith's shooting spree, Won-Joon Yoon fell victim to the same racial hatred that resulted in Byrdsong's death. Yoon was a native of South Korea, and was in the United States to receive his higher education. Upon completing his master's degree in economics at the University of Southern Illinois, he moved to Bloomington just five weeks before the shootings to begin work on his doctoral degree at Indiana University.

Won-Joon Yoon, whose family members were some of the first Christians in South Korea, was shot dead as he walked into Korean United Methodist Church. Indiana University now offers a scholarship in Yoon's memory. . . .

The Murder of an Abortion Provider

Scott Roeder, a Far Right radical who was once connected to a separatist militia called the Montana Freemen, murdered Dr. George Tiller on May 31, 2009. Tiller was one of the country's only providers of late-term abortions, a practice Roeder considered to be grounds for "justifiable homicide." While Tiller was serving as an usher at Reformation Lutheran Church in Wichita, Kansas, Roeder entered the building and gunned Tiller down with an entire congregation present.

Roeder, motivated by an "eye-for-an-eye" philosophy with regard to what he saw as the murder of unborn children, was not the first extremist to shoot Tiller. In 1993, Tiller was shot in each of his arms, and his clinic was the target of a bombing in 1985. Scott Roeder's brother stated that he "suffered from mental illness at various times in his life." Nevertheless, he was able to obtain a gun and use it to commit this hate-driven murder.

The Attack of an Army Recruiting Station

Hate shootings are not limited to churches or right-wing extremists. On June 1, 2009, a terrorist named Abdulhakim Mujahid Muhammad, an American citizen and native of Tennessee, who was under preliminary investigation by the FBI's [Federal Bureau of Investigation's] Joint Terrorism Task Force, shot two United States soldiers outside a recruiting station in Little Rock, Arkansas, killing one, Private William Long. In the arrest report, Muhammad is quoted as saying that "he was mad at the U.S. military because of what they had done to Muslims in the past," and that "he would have killed more soldiers had they been in the parking lot." After police arrested him, a search of his vehicle revealed an assault rifle. Numerous killers have armed themselves with assault weapons, particularly when they undertake assaults on mass numbers of people or where they are likely to have to respond to authorities.

Muhammad had recently been deported from Yemen to the United States for carrying a false Somali passport, but he still had easy access to guns. At the time of his arrest, Muhammad was also in possession of a .22-caliber rifle, a .380-caliber handgun, "more than 150 rounds of ammunition for the two rifles, and an additional 24 rounds for the handgun." Also in the car were "several boxes of ammunition and a red duffle bag containing two homemade silencers, binoculars, clothing, and medicine," making it clear that Muhammad planned to go on a rampage of terror.

Muhammad was charged with capital murder and 15 counts related to terrorism in connection with the shooting, which killed Pvt. William Long. Long's father, Daris, told reporters that his son had just gotten home from basic training at Fort Benning, and said, "They weren't on the battlefield, but apparently the battlefield's here."

A Mass Police Shooting in Pennsylvania

The most deadly incident of extremist-related gun violence in 2009 occurred in April in Pittsburgh, Pennsylvania. On April 4, 2009, police were called to a domestic violence incident, and when they arrived, Richard Poplawski, a white supremacist, was "lying in wait" for them. When police arrived at the scene, Poplawski, "armed with an assault rifle and two other guns," ambushed police and kept them at bay for hours before a gunshot to the leg forced his surrender.

Poplawski believed President Barack Obama was going to institute a nationwide gun ban, and had, according to his mother, been "stockpiling guns and ammunition, buying and selling the weapons online." Poplawski did originally purchase his guns online, but to complete the sale of a weapon from an out-of-state online seller, the seller must send the gun to an in-state gun store, where the recipient can pick it up after undergoing a Brady background check. The vendor who received Poplawski's guns and subsequently sold them to him was Braverman Arms, located in the nearby town of Wilkinsburg, Pennsylvania.

Poplawski had been discharged from the Marines in 2005, reportedly for assaulting a drill sergeant, and had been subject to a protection-from-abuse order an ex-girlfriend placed against him. It is not known if the discharge was dishonorable (the Marines will only say he was discharged for a "psychological order"), which would have disqualified him from buying guns. Edward Perkovic, a friend of Poplawski's, wondered, "How did he pass those background checks? Who let him have these guns?" Poplawski also possessed a permit to carry a concealed weapon in Allegheny County, Pennsylvania, the county that is home to Pittsburgh and Wilkinsburg.

The Holocaust Memorial Museum Shooting

A decade after the Benjamin Smith shootings, another hateful attack again reminded America of what happens when extremists exploit lax gun laws. On June 10, 2009, radical white supremacist James von Brunn shot and killed security guard Stephen Johns in an attack on the United States Holocaust Memorial Museum in Washington, D.C. Von Brunn, who in 1999 wrote a book entitled *Kill the Best Gentiles*, has a long history of anti-Semitism and animosity towards the government. In 1983, he was "convicted of attempting to kidnap members of the Federal Reserve Board. He was arrested two years earlier outside the room where the board was meeting, carrying a revolver, knife, and sawed-off shotgun."

In connection with the Federal Reserve incident, von Brunn served six and a half years in prison (he was convicted of attempted kidnapping and second-degree burglary). In the time leading up to the shooting at the Holocaust Memorial Museum, von Brunn was reportedly getting more and more violent, and wrote that, "It's time to kill all the Jews."

While von Brunn's extreme right-wing beliefs motivated him to go to the Holocaust museum and start shooting, his felony conviction should have precluded him from owning or possessing the gun he used to kill Stephen Johns. It is currently unclear how von Brunn obtained this weapon, but stronger gun laws and stronger enforcement could have prevented him from possessing it at the time of the shooting. If he purchased or was given the gun after his release from prison, the sale or gift of the weapon to him was illegal. If he received the weapon before he went to prison, it was illegal for him to continue to own it after his release. California has enacted gun laws that remedy this, and would have enabled the authorities to take von Brunn's gun away from him. However, even if von Brunn's gun had been taken from him, he still would have been able to walk into a gun show and purchase a weapon with cash, no background checks, no paperwork, and no questions asked. . . .

A Wake-Up Call

The connection between hate groups and extremists and the easy availability of guns can only be ignored at our peril. Killers like James von Brunn, Richard Poplawski, and Scott Roeder, all following in the hate-filled footsteps of Benjamin Smith, have gained access to guns and killed innocent civilians, doctors, soldiers, and police. Loopholes that allow criminals and other dangerous people to obtain and retain guns all too easily—including military-style assault weapons—remain open, and are exploited by extremists.

According to the Department of Homeland Security, right-wing extremists have capitalized on the economic crisis and the election of the first African American president and are "focusing their efforts to recruit new members, mobilize existing supporters, and broaden their scope and appeal through propaganda." This resurgence of right-wing extremism makes the easy availability of guns all the more disconcerting. Although gun control legislation has succeeded in blocking 1.6 million individual gun purchases, gaping loopholes continue to make it far too easy for dangerous people to get guns. Federal law allows unlicensed sellers to sell guns without background checks, does not limit the number of handguns that traffickers can buy, and restricts law enforcement from cracking down on corrupt gun dealers. And federal law does not even prevent known or suspected terrorists from purchasing firearms unless they have already committed a crime. Lone-wolf extremists, armed with pistols, shotguns, rifles, and assault rifles, are "harder to stop, harder to know about, [and] much more difficult to defend against" than the average large-scale terrorist organization, and are capable of causing as many deaths and inspiring as much fear as international terrorist networks.

The Big Lie

Despite the glaring atrocities committed in recent years by gun-wielding extremists, the NRA still uses its political might to advocate policies that make it easier to sell guns to dangerous people and that place our families and loved ones at risk. And the gun lobby all too often has engaged in inflammatory and dangerous rhetoric that may fan the flames of hate among extremists. The NRA and others in the gun lobby continue to propagate the "big lie"—that President Obama is intent on taking away the guns of law-abiding gun owners. This assertion may be good for maintaining NRA membership dues and ginning up gun sales, but it is an utter fabrication. . . .

The fact that racist spree killer Benjamin Smith was able to obtain his guns from a trafficker supplied by a corrupt dealer shows the need for stronger gun laws—requiring background checks for all gun sales, limiting bulk handgun sales, and giving law enforcement the tools to crack down on corrupt gun dealers. In defense of their opposition to these commonsense proposals, the NRA likes to say that "guns don't kill people, people kill people." However, in the words of *New York Times* columnist Bob Herbert, while we cannot blame the NRA for these specific acts of violence, we "can sure blame it for ignoring the tragic lessons of history and continuing to spray gasoline into an environment that we have seen explode time and again." Through our weak gun laws, we are making it easy for people to kill people—with guns. Washington must put the safety of the American people ahead of the desires of the gun lobby, and should enact the strong, commonsense laws we need to keep dangerous weapons out of the hands of dangerous people.

> *"Popular culture, through violent film, music and video games, often glorifies the use of arms."*

Popular Culture Promotes Gun Violence

Dariusz Dziewanski

Studies show that social and cultural forces prompt some people to turn to gun violence, claims Dariusz Dziewanski in the following viewpoint. Pop culture images lead some young people to believe that wielding guns can lead to affluence and power, he asserts. Indeed, Dziewanski maintains, guns are often associated with other symbols of success in popular culture such as expensive cars, jewelry, and sexually available women. For poor, marginalized youth who see few roads to advancement, guns have a potent appeal, he reasons. Dziewanski works for the Canadian International Development Agency, whose mission is to reduce poverty and promote economic equity.

As you read, consider the following questions:

1. According to an author quoted in the viewpoint, how do media create the perception that more crime exists, when crime is actually decreasing?

Dariusz Dziewanski, "Young Guns," *Briar Patch*, vol. 37, September–October 2008, pp. 23–26. Reproduced by permission.

2. What reasons did Ottawa gang members give for carrying guns?

3. What are some of the risk factors that the Small Arms Survey identified in a 2006 article?

"The first gun I bought was from a friend of a friend—a 35 [millimeter]. I had held pistols before, but finally had my own. I was 16 and remember staring down the barrel like I was going to shoot. But I had never fired one before and if somebody had shot at me, I wouldn't have known how to shoot back.

"I was fine to just show it around and act tough. It made me feel respected."

So says a former Ottawa gang member, recalling a misspent childhood among guns and gangs. Six-foot-two, tattooed and wearing a baggy track suit, this imposing stereotype of a self-proclaimed criminal is quick to laugh at himself now as he tells stories about his past. "I was badass," he says, "but I was also totally scared."

Social and Cultural Forces

While most violent crimes in Canada are committed with knives, clubs and other blunt instruments, firearms do contribute to social violence in certain contexts, especially among young males. In particular, there is growing empirical evidence that social and cultural forces influence whether or not an individual turns to armed violence. Despite overall drops in overall violent gun crime in Canada, a national fixation on guns is intensifying among youth, and this growing trend is being fuelled by media and pop culture.

Violence, particularly gun violence, can be learned. As young men take lessons from the world around them, some appear to relate to violent imagery, as it justifies and even glorifies their own use of arms.

Although the vast majority of youth in Canada are not turning to guns, some are identifying with a pop culture of violence that leads them to believe that guns are their ticket to affluence and power. Caught between the material world and the real world, young men in impoverished neighbourhoods pick up firearms hoping to defend themselves against a form of structural violence that kills people slowly through alienation, exclusion and marginalization. Perceptions are reality, and in their world the perception is (as the NRA [National Rifle Association of America] is so fond of saying) that an armed person is a citizen, while an unarmed person is merely a subject.

The Marginalized Youth-Violence Connection

A February 2008 Statistics Canada report entitled "Firearms and Violent Crime" revealed that more Canadian youth are using guns when committing acts of violent crime. While the report also points to a 30-year low in overall violent gun crime, the percentage of youth aged 12 to 17 years accused of a firearm-related violent crime is at its highest point since 1998. The percentage of adolescents accused of homicide in 2006 is higher than it has been in over three decades, with more getting involved in serious criminal activity at a younger age, often as members of gangs in urban centres.

Christian Pearce is the co-authour of the book *Enter the Babylon System*, an exploration of the emerging gun culture in North America. "Once guns are present and combined with poverty," he says, "they become problematic. Youth are not inherently violent, but are often marginalized and scared. In neighborhoods with violence, youth often feel threatened, even by police. That's when they turn to guns." This seems to be particularly so when young men are excluded from non-violent avenues of advancement, or if they face discrimination or threats to their security. This is not to say that armed violence is a reasonable or constructive response to marginalization, but in these situations, violence can have a powerful appeal.

As Pearce points out, "media jumps on criminal activity as entertainment and creates the perception that there is more crime, when crime is actually decreasing." The day after the aforementioned Statistics Canada report, stories of youth and guns dominated news headlines, with low overall gun crime reduced to a subplot. That seems fair enough. Armed youth violence is a problem that should be reported, discussed and addressed—but not in a way that sensationalizes the issue, or leads to what Pearce calls the "demonization" of youth, which is what tends to happen. In his opinion, this message is "simplistic and archaic" and creates a self-fulfilling prophecy. Instead, more must be done to "believe in, respect and invest in youth."

Anti-Social Capital

Part of the problem, according to James Sheptycki, a professor of criminology at York University, is that the public discussion of these issues, and of their potential solutions, too often falls into blind ideology and polarizing extremes. "Far too much complexity is lost," Sheptycki says. "More nuanced discussion must emerge if the policies developed to tackle gun crime are to be effective." Perhaps this lack of nuance stems in part from the news media's bad-news-first policy, or the reporting of stories painted in sweeping strokes. Maybe it is that guns represent a politically charged topic that is often reduced to easily digestible, largely meaningless slogans like "guns don't kill people, people do."

The city of Ottawa distinguishes itself as both a scene of youth gang violence and, potentially, at least, a source of leadership in the efforts to reduce such violence. In October 2007, the federal government's Throne Speech identified "tackling crime," particularly violent gun crime, as one of its key priorities. The government translated these promises into Bill C-2, which, among other measures, seeks tougher minimum prison sentences for serious gun crimes that involve restricted or prohibited weapons or are connected with gangs, as well as longer sentences for other gun crimes like trafficking and smuggling. In addition, the bill also proposes that youth charged with violent crimes, including gun crimes, be tried as adults. Although some, especially victim groups, applaud the Tories [political party] for their tough stance on gun crime, many see these efforts as counterproductive. "You can't incarcerate your way out of gun crime," argues Ottawa University Criminology Professor Irvin Waller. "There must be an effort made to address the sources of gun violence, by building safety through prevention."

Meanwhile, the city of Ottawa boasts an estimated 600 gang members, typically concentrated in low-income, high-density communities in the city's Greenbelt. Gang membership in the city is often linked to guns. In an effort to give a face to a problem that has typically been reduced to statistics and stereotypes, I arranged to sit down with three former gang members from east Ottawa.

Protection and Respect

When asked why they carried guns, each cited protection and respect as their main reasons. "If you shoot it or not, you've got respect and feel like you do not have to take anything from anybody," said one of the former gang members. He had been in the gang until only recently, and still displayed the boyish antagonism of somebody who is used to being threatened. Violence, including armed violence, can be a powerful form of self-preservation, both physically and psychologically. Those living in poor or dangerous areas feel a continual threat to their personal safety.

Of the three youth, all had owned firearms at some point, but only one admitted to actually shooting at another person,

Signals That Violence Is Acceptable

Children are spoon-fed that, under certain conditions, violence is acceptable. They see it through the movies they watch, most of which are aimed at young people; they see it through the television programs geared to their age group; they hear violence glorified through their music; and they are taught that violence can be entertaining in their video games. They receive signals through every aspect of life that violence has a place in society and that it is okay to do certain things. All learning is environmental. We owe it to all children . . . to teach them that violence is not acceptable under any circumstance.

Joseph Q. Davis,
"The Legacy of 'If Someone Hits You, You Better Hit Back,'"
Reclaiming Children and Youth, *Spring 2006.*

in what he called "revenge for the beating of a friend." By his own admission, however, he "didn't even come close" to hitting anybody. The same young man had also been shot at, and all three said that they knew both perpetrators and victims of shootings.

The young man who cited respect as being a motivating factor for carrying a weapon was also quick to point out that he had "had a gun, but for a long time didn't have bullets." The oldest son of Somali immigrants, he, like the other two interviewees, seemed to fluctuate awkwardly between being tough and being scared. In one instance, an emphatic story of a robbery faded into the recollection of his heartbroken mother who "cried at the news that her son had been arrested."

Images of Guns and Success

The mythology in our culture surrounding the display and use of guns is powerful, indeed. According to Sheptycki, "there are powerful cultural forces that create a mythology around gun use, creating a pathway to criminality. Popular culture, through violent film, music and video games, often glorifies the use of arms. Some hip hop, for example, endorses profligacy and violence. Its speech and mannerisms are often intentionally threatening, and endorse socioeconomic ascension through violent means."

Generally, adolescent males are the main consumers of music that features firearm violence and movies loaded with armed violent scenes. They also are the principal targets for violent video games, especially first-person shooter games, which render the experience of killing from the perspective of the player character and within which a gun is often the preferred means of violence. The youths most prone to armed violence, in particular those who perceive success to be inaccessible through nonviolent means, may be the same ones who tend to identify with these popular representations of gun violence.

Pop culture frequently associates firearms with other popular symbols of male success, including expensive cars, designer clothing, jewellery and scantily clad, sexually available women. On a daily basis, the have-nots are riddled with media messages of what they should have. The hip-hop lifestyle, for example, is itself branded: Cristal champagne, Mercedes cars and Versace clothing are all a part of this, coexisting alongside gun brands such as Glock or Smith & Wesson. Guns are a commodity in consumer culture and are advertised through songs, music videos, and movies, along with other items portrayed as symbols of affluence.

"You see a guy with a gun, you see him in a car, wearing a gold chain and nice kicks—and especially girls. Why wouldn't I want that?" explained one 20-year-old former gang member.

Though now unarmed, he still confidently displays a gold chain and expensive shoes, presumably for the same reasons he used to carry a gun. When asked if he could attain such a lifestyle without a gun, he responded, "sure, lots of people don't have guns: janitors don't have guns, garbagemen don't have guns. Whatever, they don't have money, cars, or girls either."

Simply possessing a gun can make a man appear powerful, rich and strong. Marginalized young males frequently lack power, despite being socially conditioned to seek it. Masculinity, at least as it is defined in popular culture, is deeply invested in a search for power and status, increasing the desire to "weaponize" in order to counter any perceived emasculation.

Facing the Risk Factors

That is not to say that all young men who are exposed to hip hop, guns, or even poverty will turn to violent crime. Many more youth who face the same risk factors are reluctant to participate in delinquency or violence. According to Youth Services Ottawa, the vast majority of young men with whom they are involved are nonviolent and are just trying to meet their basic needs. "Pop culture and poverty affect more than just gang members and those that take up arms," says Dennis Rodgers, a lecturer in Urban Development at the London School of Economics. Through his research on violence, he has come to the opinion that "no study has ever managed to predict on a precise level what would predispose somebody to gang activity and armed crime." But in general terms, research initiatives have identified several risk factors that do predispose young men to armed violence. In their 2006 article "Angry Young Men," the Small Arms Survey, an independent research project based in Geneva, identified a number of these risk factors, including: being labelled as troublesome, low school achievement, having witnessed or experienced violence in the home or community, limited parental control, holding more traditional or rigid views about gender, and having used violence and seen that violence produces respect. A recognition that these risk factors exist can inform effective policies which will help to reduce gun violence—not just among youth, but overall.

The Small Arms Survey has also identified a number of protective social factors that can safeguard some young men from becoming involved in crime and violence. These include having valued and stable relationships with people whom they would disappoint by becoming involved in armed violence, being aware of the risks associated with the violent version of masculinity, and finding alternative male peer groups that provide positive reinforcement for nonviolent male identities.

Examining Preventative Measures

A February 2008 report by Crime Prevention Ottawa on youth gang prevention in the city pointed to a number of initiatives to encourage these and other protective factors among at-risk youth. Life-skills development, after-school programs, organized sports, academic support and mentoring and parent support programs are hardly glamorous, but they are the first line of preventative defence against armed criminality. Research and interviews suggest that when it comes to the long-term solutions to gun violence among youth, prevention is the name of the game, particularly the introduction of comprehensive initiatives that seek to both promote protective factors and remove risk factors.

According to the Small Arms Survey, it is also critical to reshape social symbolism surrounding guns and disarm the pop culture of violence. This requires a broad cultural shift in which media and pop culture can play a key role. In some instances, celebrities have stepped up to raise awareness and serve as positive role models. In a 2007 interview with the *Toronto Star*, Christian Pearce described how a hip-hop artist like Canada's Solitair can write a song like "Easy to Slip" about a cousin who lived a gangster lifestyle and was shot dead as a result. The song begins with the artist looking up to his older 16-year-old cousin for the "gold chains, Nike Air Jordans, chicks on his jock", but ends in a warning against a violent life: "I ain't a hustler, my cousin packed a gun, and his memory's the reason I will never pack one."

Similarly, the rhymes of Toronto's k-os focus on promoting a positive message, while at times expressing criticism of mainstream hip-hop culture's obsession with money, fame and glorification of violence. Just as media, pop culture, or hip hop can contribute to the gun problem, they can also play a powerful role in contributing to peaceful solutions. Solitair and k-os are examples of celebrities who can project a positive masculine ideal that is successful, admirable, and attractive, and that rejects gun violence.

A Collective Effort

While gun use is often seen as a male problem that men need to take responsibility for confronting, women can play an important role in promoting peace. For instance, in Colombia, women living in the violence-ridden city of Pereira joined the local government's disarmament efforts in a so-called "crossed legs" initiative that saw participating women withholding sex from husbands and boyfriends who refused to get rid of their weapons. Of course, the fostering of healthier gender relations and less destructive ideals of masculinity requires a much broader empowerment of women than the selective withholding of sex from male partners engaged in violence. Nevertheless, this example demonstrates that women are vital to, and can be successful in, promoting nonviolence among men, even in the world's most violent settings.

Indeed, reducing gun violence is a collective effort, and one that begins with a willingness to believe in young people. In part, this means recognizing that those affected by youth crime shouldn't be simply labelled either criminals or victims. All of the youth interviewed for this [viewpoint], for instance, were at one point either direct or indirect victims as well as perpetrators of gun crime. All became involved with guns through gangs for protection, status and power. At the same time, all have mentioned that, to varying degrees of success, they are trying to "grow up" and grow into new identities less rooted in violence. All are articulate and expressive young men with hopes and aspirations, living in a world that seldom lives up to what pop culture promises. As the oldest of the three told me, "living like a gangster is easy. Anyone can beat somebody up, or carry a gun. Going to school or getting a job, that's hard. Not turning to violence or gangs, that deserves respect."

| "Violence flows through the American
  bloodstream."

America's Violent Culture Advances Gun Violence

Andrew Stephen

American young people are exposed to an alarming amount of violence on an ever-increasing array of technology, argues Andrew Stephen in the following viewpoint. To compensate for being the most indulged generation in history, American youth create unrealistic self-images of masculinity, he maintains. When those who do not outgrow the obsession with violent video games have easy access to weapons, the result is often tragic, Stephen asserts. Sadly, he claims, pundits who have never themselves been under fire blame everything but America's culture of violence. Stephen is U.S. editor of the New Statesman, *a British newsmagazine.*

As you read, consider the following questions:

1. According to Stephen, what do Americans adamantly brush aside?

2. What are the most sought after videos on YouTube?

Andrew Stephen, "The Unmentionable Causes of Violence," *New Statesman*, vol. 136, April 30, 2007, pp. 20–21. Copyright © 2007 New Statesman, Ltd. Reproduced by permission.

3. What did Mark Steyn claim prevented students at Virginia Tech from subduing Cho Seung-Hui?

If there was anything unique about Cho Seung-Hui [also known as Seung-Hui Cho, the Virginia Tech student who killed 33 people, including himself, on April 16, 2007], it wasn't that he was a paranoid schizophrenic armed with Walther .22 and 9mm Glock pistols and driven by unfathomable torment and rage. The rest of the world understands very well that mental illness and the easy availability of guns have made for a lethal combination throughout American history, and will continue to do so for the foreseeable future. The endlessly repeated statistics of domestic death and mayhem, which most Americans still adamantly brush aside, tell their own story.

A Product of 21st-Century Technology

What singled out Cho Seung-Hui was that he was the first post-YouTube, Facebook, MySpace and IM [instant message] disaffected youth of his kind—a product of 21st-century technology, rather than just that of the 20th. From his addiction to a ghastly, violent video game called *Counter-Strike* in his teens, he had moved on: He knew exactly how to produce 28 QuickTime video clips and 43 photos of himself, aware that by sending them to NBC, his first and last moments of stardom would not only reach the MM (as the mainstream media are nowadays derisively called by his generation), but would also be flashed around the world in seconds via YouTube and the like, allowing him to leave his own brief but indelible mark on history. Manifestly delusional though he may have been, he knew exactly how to look a camera in the eye and address it like a pro.

Never before, in fact, have young Americans been so bombarded with images of violence, a trend that is alarming mental health specialists. Dr Mark Mills, a distinguished forensic psychiatrist who has written extensively on the subject for publications such as the *American Journal of Psychiatry*, tells me: "The thing that has changed ... is that anybody wanting to see violence can now see it." Films of the execution of Saddam Hussein and the beheadings of hostages in Iraq, for example, are still the images on YouTube (which had 6,030 clips of Saddam's execution available last Monday [April 2007]) that are most sought after by young Americans.

I know not just kids addicted to such video games in the way Cho Seung-Hui was, but younger *teachers*, too. For the overwhelming majority, the craze passes and video games and online surfing become harmless. A 17-year-old I know, for instance, logged on at the appointed 5 P.M. a few days ago to learn whether his (online) college application had been successful. He immediately phoned a girlfriend to give her his news, and within 15 seconds a mutual friend had logged in to his Facebook page to congratulate him. Less than a minute later, a cousin across the continent in California had chimed in: a generation permanently texting and socialising online, but in a nation besotted with violence.

An Unparalleled Danger

Therein lies the unparalleled danger for the US, one that does not apply to any other Western country whose young people have similarly easy access to the Internet. Violence flows through the American bloodstream. The craze never passed for 23-year-old Cho Seung-Hui.

Present-day American males are the most primped and pampered examples of their species in history, and compensate by vicariously nurturing self-images of masculinity that are removed from reality. Hence the ready availability of their would-be macho guns and most Americans' refusal to face the blindingly obvious: that the Virginia Tech tragedy would never have happened had Cho Seung-Hui not been able to walk into an all-American gun shop called Roanoke Firearms and walk

away minutes later with his Glock and 50 rounds of ammunition for $571 (or log on to eBay, as he later did, to buy magazines for more ammo).

Men in Denial

I was sitting around a lunch table with a group of television executives a couple of days after the shootings, and the talk centred entirely around whether NBC was right to air Cho's rants. Nobody brought up the unmentionable subject of the availability of guns, and I chickened out from doing so. The US media (and practically every leading Democrat) have skipped and danced and weaved around the subject, ending up transfixed like rabbits in headlights. The *Washington Post* had 75 reporters on the story within minutes—I'm not exaggerating—but you could learn more from one British report in the *Sunday Times*, say, than from the *Post*'s convoluted coverage.

Thus, 21st-century American men who have never been under fire themselves, or even heard a shot fired in anger, inevitably became the most vociferous cheerleaders for what is actually mass denial. Bill O'Reilly, the current resident clown-in-chief of Fox News, told viewers that it was "the Far Left" calling for gun control. My erstwhile opposite number on the *Spectator*, Mark Steyn, thought that a wimpy new "culture of passivity" had stopped the poor kids at Virginia Tech from somehow storming and subduing Cho. It is "this awful corrosive passivity", rather than "the psycho killer", said Steyn, writing in the *National Review*, that is the real threat to the nation.

Dream on, America.

Periodical Bibliography

The following articles have been selected to supplement the diverse views presented in this chapter.

Joseph Q. Davis "The Legacy of 'If Someone Hits You, You Better Hit Back,'" *Reclaiming Children and Youth*, Spring 2006.

Charlie Gillis "American Guns, Canadian Violence," *Maclean's*, August 15, 2005.

Kristin A. Goss "Good Policy, Not Stories, Can Reduce Violence," *Chronicle of Higher Education*, vol. 53, no. 35, May 2007.

Bob Herbert "A Threat We Can't Ignore," *New York Times*, June 20, 2009.

A. Barton Hinkle "Armed Citizens: Both Left and Right Could Use Second Amendment Refresher," *Richmond Times-Dispatch*, June 26, 2009.

Darcus Howe "Hot-Headed Murders That Can Be Stopped," *New Statesman*, April 7, 2008.

Jackson Katz "Memo to the Media: It's Men's Violence," *Voice Male*, Winter 2007.

Jordan Michael Smith "Crimes and Misconceptions," *Western Standard* (Vancouver, British Columbia, Canada), July 30, 2007.

Will Sullivan "An Uphill Climb for Gun Laws; A New Debate, Perhaps, but the Same Old Politics," *U.S. News & World Report*, April 30, 2007.

Washington Times "God or Guns?" April 23, 2009.

OPPOSING
VIEWPOINTS®
SERIES

CHAPTER 3

Do Private Gun
Ownership Policies
Reduce Gun Violence?

Chapter Preface

In 1994, to settle a domestic violence complaint made against him by his wife Mary Ann during a contentious divorce, Randy Edward Hayes of West Virginia pled guilty to misdemeanor battery and was sentenced to one year of probation. Ten years later, during a dispute over visitation rights with their son, police responded to another domestic violence call from his wife. Typically, Hayes would have faced a similar charge that might have been resolved with a similar plea and probation. However, a deputy sheriff found a rifle under Randy Hayes's bed. Hayes was then indicted for a much more serious crime, a violation of the Gun Ban for Individuals Convicted of a Misdemeanor Crime of Domestic Violence, also known as the Lautenberg Amendment, named after its sponsor, Senator Frank Lautenberg of New Jersey. Like many private gun ownership policies, the Lautenberg Amendment is subject to rigorous debate.

Those who support the Lautenberg Amendment argue that the law helps reduce the tragic link between guns and domestic violence deaths. According to the activist organization Legal Momentum, between a thousand and sixteen hundred women die each year at the hands of their male partners, and when domestic abusers have a gun, they are twelve times more likely to kill their victims. Guns in the hands of domestic violence abusers also pose a threat to police officers. According to the Brady Center to Prevent Gun Violence, 14 percent of all police officer deaths occur during domestic violence calls. In fact, claims Ladd Everitt, "most reasonable Americans would agree that a man who beats a woman doesn't have the right to own a firearm"[1] The Gun Control Act of 1968 prohibits felons from owning guns. However, in some

---

1. Quoted in Katie Gaughan, "Should Domestic Violence Abusers Own Guns?" Campus Progress, December 2008. www.campusprogress.org.

states, domestic violence remains a misdemeanor. The Lautenberg Amendment closes this loophole.

Opponents of the amendment argue that the law denies the Second Amendment right to keep and bear arms. In fact, criminal defense lawyers nationwide who seek to nullify Lautenberg Amendment convictions cite *District of Columbia v. Heller*. This 2008 Supreme Court decision for the first time judicially recognized the Second Amendment right to own a gun for purposes of self-defense in the home. Ohio State University law professor Douglas Berman argues, "*Heller* at the very least can and should be read as the vindication of those subject to harsh sanctions for gun possession to raise new constitutional questions to get around them."[2] Others argue that the ban is unconstitutional because it is too broad. The gun rights organization Gun Owners of America claims, "Under the Lautenberg ban, people who have committed very minor offenses that include pushing, shoving or, in some cases, merely yelling at a family member can no longer own a firearm for self-defense."[3] In fact, Hayes's attorney appealed the conviction, and the U.S. Court of Appeals for the Fourth Circuit vacated Hayes's felon-in-possession conviction in April 2007, arguing that the Lautenberg law only barred gun possession by abusers convicted of laws specifically barring domestic violence.

The U.S. Supreme Court, however, reversed the federal appeals court ruling in February 2009 by a vote of 7 to 2. The court backed the Lautenberg Amendment as a reasonable restriction on private gun ownership rights. Nevertheless, opponents continue to challenge the law. The authors in the following chapter explore other controversies concerning which private gun ownership polices are best. Commentators on both sides of the issue will continue to inform this debate.

---

2. Quoted in Kenneth Jost, "Gun Rights Debates," *CQ Researcher*, October 31, 2008.
3. Ibid.

> *"Stronger laws and policies . . . will protect our families and communities from gun violence by making it harder for . . . prohibited persons to obtain guns."*

Laws Controlling Private Gun Ownership Will Reduce Gun Violence

Brady Campaign to Prevent Gun Violence

Laws regulating private gun ownership have been reducing crime since 1993, maintains the Brady Campaign to Prevent Gun Violence in the following viewpoint. Unfortunately, some laws have lapsed, and the gun lobby has weakened the effectiveness of others, the campaign asserts. To reduce gun violence, the campaign argues, laws should extend background checks to all gun sales, block the sale of guns to those on the terrorist watch list, and prohibit large-volume handgun sales. Sarah and Jim Brady founded the campaign after Jim was shot in 1981 in an assassination attempt on President Ronald Reagan.

Gun Violence in America: Proposals for the Obama Administration. Washington, DC: Brady Campaign to Prevent Gun Violence, 2008. Copyright © 2008 Brady Center to Prevent Gun Violence. Reproduced by permission.

As you read, consider the following questions:

1. What nation is the sole high-income, industrialized country that has not addressed the problem of gun violence?

2. Through what backdoor method do millions of firearms change hands every year, in Eric Holder's opinion?

3. What do federal law enforcement authorities claim indicates that a buyer intends to traffic guns to the illegal market?

America's gun violence problem must be addressed if we are to effectively respond to the crises facing our health care system, urban communities, and homeland security. In this country, it is too easy for dangerous people to obtain dangerous weapons. There are only a few federal gun laws, and even those have loopholes. This leads to senseless gun deaths and injuries affecting thousands each year. We should implement stronger laws and policies that will protect our families and communities from gun violence by making it harder for convicted felons, the dangerously mentally ill, and other prohibited persons to obtain guns.

The Problem of Gun Violence

Every day in America, guns claim 84 lives, and wound nearly 200; every year more than 30,000 people die—over 3,000 of them children and teens—and over 70,000 are injured. Firearm homicide is the leading cause of death for black men ages 15–34, and is the leading cause of death for *all* African Americans 15–24. Homicide represents the second leading cause of death for Hispanics between the ages of 15 and 24, 76% of which are firearm related. Estimates of direct medical costs for firearm injuries range from $2.3 billion to $4 billion, with additional annual indirect costs estimated at $19 billion.

America is the sole high-income, industrialized country that has not responsibly addressed the problem of gun violence. The firearms death rate in the U.S. is *eight* times higher than in other high-income countries and the rate among children under 15 years old is nearly *twelve* times higher in the U.S. than in 25 other industrialized countries *combined.*

There are effective solutions that can reduce gun violence. Beginning with the Brady Law [Brady Handgun Violence Prevention Act] in 1993, the assault weapon ban in 1994, and other [Bill] Clinton administration policies, our nation experienced an historic decline in gun crime and violence. During the first ten years of the Brady Law gun homicides dropped 37%, while other gun crimes dropped 73%. However, during the [George W.] Bush years, gun crime increased as the administration and Congress weakened the Brady Law, allowed the assault weapons ban to expire, gave the gun industry special legal protection, and instituted other counterproductive policies. . . .

Moving Forward to Prevent Gun Violence

In addition to reversing the negative legislation and policies enacted during the Bush years, the new administration and Congress should implement an affirmative agenda of legislation and regulatory reform to reduce crime and gun violence. . . .

Extend Brady Background Checks to All Gun Sales, Including All Gun Show Sales

We agree with the [Barack] Obama transition agenda that the gun show loophole should be closed, and with attorney general nominee Eric Holder that background checks should be required for all gun sales. *Our national gun policy should be "no background check, no gun, no excuses."*

The Brady Law's background check requirement has been very effective at blocking dangerous people from buying guns. Through the end of 2007, more than 1.6 million prohibited purchasers—felons, the mentally ill, domestic violence abusers, and others—have been denied sales at licensed gun dealers. However, as Holder wrote in 2001:

> Unfortunately, unlicensed sellers are permitted by law to sell firearms with no background check whatsoever. Millions of firearms change hands every year through this backdoor, yet perfectly legal, method—giving criminals and terrorists remarkably easy and undetectable access to weapons. This legal loophole must be closed immediately. We can no longer allow the purchase of firearms through the Internet or a newspaper ad, at a gun show or a flea market, or in any other type of sale from an unlicensed seller, without any background check or other record of purchase. The stakes are too high.

The no-check loophole is a major supply source for criminals who want guns, especially at gun shows. It is estimated that about 40% of gun sales are made by unlicensed sellers.

Eighteen states and the District of Columbia have taken steps to close the "gun show loophole," with several requiring background checks on all gun sales. Model legislation has worked since 1989 in California, where every gun sale must first be run through the state's background check system. Unlicensed sellers need only take their guns to a licensed dealer to run the check and complete the sale.

Background checks should be required for all gun sales.

Fully Fund the NICS Improvement Act

On January 8, 2008, President Bush signed into law the National Instant [Criminal Background] Check System (NICS) Improvement Amendments Act of 2007, which provides for financial assistance to aid states in sending records to NICS and financial penalties if they fail to provide records. This law was passed after the Virginia Tech massacre, where the killer was able to arm himself because a court order that should have blocked his gun purchase was not reported to NICS. In response, some states have reviewed their records and procedures and started forwarding more records to the

NICS. But more progress will be possible if Congress appropriates the funds authorized by the Act.

The NICS system was first implemented in 1998, as required by the Brady Law, to ensure that prohibited purchasers cannot buy firearms from gun dealers. However, a background check is only as good as the records it can search. Many prohibited persons are not blocked from buying guns because their records are not in NICS, including about 80–90% of relevant mental health records and 25% of felony convictions. A fully funded NICS Act should help block hundreds of thousands of prohibited buyers who are not presently stopped by the Brady Law because their names are not in NICS.

Congress should appropriate the full amount of authorized funding to assist states in submitting records of prohibited purchasers to NICS.

Close the "Terror Gap" to Deny Firearms to Terrorists

Under current law, known or suspected terrorists are not prohibited from buying or possessing firearms, unless they have already committed crimes or are otherwise barred. As attorney general nominee Eric Holder wrote in 2001, there are "numerous and chilling examples" of terrorists buying guns in America, and there are many more recent examples as well.

One solution was proposed by Senator Frank Lautenberg (D-NJ) and Representative Peter King (R-NY) in the "Denying Firearms and Explosives to Dangerous Terrorists Act." Based on a Bush administration proposal, this legislation would provide the U.S. attorney general [AG] with discretionary authority to block a gun sale to a known or suspected terrorist where the AG reasonably believes that the person may use a firearm or explosives in connection with terrorism. In 2001, Holder called for background checks to include "whether the potential buyer is on an FBI [Federal Bureau of Investigation] or other law enforcement watch list of suspected terrorists." Incoming Chief of Staff Rahm Emanuel has strongly endorsed terror gap legislation.

The "terror gap" loophole should be closed.

Prohibit Gun Possession by Violent Misdemeanants and Persons Convicted of Violent Acts as Juveniles

Criminals who have been convicted of certain violent misdemeanors are not barred from gun possession under current law. This loophole should be closed. A study found that persons convicted of violent misdemeanors were eight times more likely to be charged with subsequent firearm and/or violent crimes, and one out of every three violent misdemeanants who sought to buy handguns were arrested for new crimes within three years of buying the handgun. As attorney general nominee Eric Holder has advocated, we should also close the loophole that allows persons convicted of violent and other serious offenses as juveniles to legally purchase a weapon on their 18th birthday or later in adulthood.

A law should be enacted to bar gun possession by individuals who have been convicted of certain violent misdemeanors and by individuals who have been adjudicated delinquent for an act that would have been a violent felony if committed by an adult.

Strengthen ATF Authority

Restrict Large-Volume Handgun Sales to Reduce Trafficking

Large-volume handgun sales should be restricted as part of a comprehensive strategy to reduce gun violence. Even though high-volume handgun sales facilitate gun trafficking into the illegal market, current federal law allows any legal purchaser to buy an unlimited number of handguns in a single purchase.

Gun traffickers often buy large numbers of handguns to resell to criminals. Handguns sold in multiple sales accounted for 20% of all handguns sold and traced to crime in 2000. For example, one Ohio gun dealer sold hundreds of guns at gun shows to a gun trafficking ring—including 87 handguns in a single transaction. The guns were trafficked from Ohio into New York State, where they have been used in dozens of

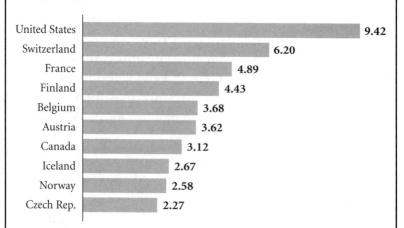

U.S. Ranks Highest in Gun Deaths

The U.S. has the highest rate of gun deaths among some of the world's richest nations.

United States	9.42
Switzerland	6.20
France	4.89
Finland	4.43
Belgium	3.68
Austria	3.62
Canada	3.12
Iceland	2.67
Norway	2.58
Czech Rep.	2.27

Worst gun death rates per 100,000 population, 2004 (Includes homicide, suicide, accidental and undetermined deaths)

TAKEN FROM: Small Arms Survey, Geneva Associated Press.

crimes. Federal law enforcement authorities have long regarded the purchase of multiple handguns by a single buyer in a single transaction as an "indicator" that the buyer intends to traffic the guns to the illegal market. For this reason, if someone buys two or more handguns in a five-day period, federal law treats the purchase as suspect, and it must be reported to ATF [Bureau of Alcohol, Tobacco, Firearms, and Explosives].

Congress should enact a law similar to those enacted in California, Maryland, and Virginia, restricting handgun purchases to one per month per purchaser. A Brady Center [to Prevent Gun Violence] study published in the *Journal of the American Medical Association* found that Virginia's law reduced crime guns trafficked from Virginia; before the law, 38% of guns originating in the Southeast and traced in the

Northeast were sold in Virginia, but after the law Virginia's share was reduced to 16%. However, because gun traffickers can use new "source" states when a state law is enacted, a federal law is needed.

A federal law restricting bulk handgun sales should be enacted.

Give ATF Stronger and More Flexible Authority to Enforce the Law Against Corrupt Dealers

Legislation is needed to repeal restrictions that prevent ATF from more effectively enforcing gun laws. Almost 60% of the nation's guns traced to crime come from only about 1% of the country's gun dealers, yet ATF is severely hindered in its ability to inspect, sanction, or shut down rogue dealers. The bureau's authority to revoke dealer licenses should be strengthened and it should be given new authority to inspect dealers more frequently, temporarily suspend dealer licenses, levy civil penalties, and bring felony charges against dealers for record-keeping violations that often occur when dealers engage in off-the-books gun sales.

Weak gun laws continually prevent ATF from promptly shutting down lawbreaking dealers despite years of federal gun law violations. Restrictions enacted in 1986 as part of the gun lobby–backed Firearm Owners' Protection Act ("FOPA") placed severe constraints on ATF's ability to enforce the law, including: requiring years of repeated violations before ATF can revoke the license of a corrupt gun dealer; limiting ATF's inspection powers to a single, unannounced inspection of a gun dealer in any 12-month period; classifying serious violations of firearms record-keeping laws as misdemeanors rather than felonies; and imposing a heightened "willfulness" burden of proof for most gun law violations.

Congress should enact legislation to give ATF the authority and flexibility it needs to enforce our nation's gun laws and crack down on corrupt gun dealers.

8

Strengthen ATF's Ability to Crack Down on Gun Dealers Who Sell to Straw Purchasers

Under current law, dealers can be prosecuted for engaging in sales to "straw buyers" only by relying on charges of aiding and abetting a false statement by the purchaser, or for record-keeping violations that were felonies prior to 1986 but are now classified as misdemeanors. Since federal prosecutors generally do not expend their limited resources prosecuting misdemeanors, most dealers caught violating federal law usually escape criminal prosecution. The lack of criminal prosecutions of gun dealers dramatically skews the incentives when dealers are faced with gun traffickers offering cash for firearms, leading many to make the illegal sale.

Congress should enact legislation making it a felony for any licensed dealer to transfer a firearm knowing that the person completing the paperwork is not the actual purchaser.

Require Gun Owners to Report Lost or Stolen Guns

Federal law should require gun owners to report in a timely manner missing or stolen guns to federal authorities. This is needed to prevent gun owners from covering up sales to prohibited purchasers by later claiming—when those guns are traced to crime—that their guns were stolen. ATF has reported that in 88% of the firearms traced to crime, the purchaser of the gun is not the same person as the criminal from whom the gun is recovered. While some of these guns may have been stolen from gun owners, often they were sold in the criminal market. Without a reporting requirement, it is difficult to rebut a trafficker's false claim that a gun was stolen.

Federal law already requires gun dealers to report lost or stolen firearms. Several states, including Connecticut, Massachusetts, New York, Ohio, and Rhode Island, as well as the District of Columbia, require owners to report lost or stolen guns.

Federal law should require that gun owners promptly report lost or stolen guns.

Require Licensed Dealers to Adopt Minimum Security Safeguards to Prevent Gun Thefts

A 2008 Brady Center analysis showed that, in 2007, more than 30,000 guns were reported missing from licensed gun dealers' shops. To prevent guns from being stolen by criminals, ATF should issue regulations requiring dealers to meet specified security standards in order to obtain, and retain, a license to sell guns. This could be done by ATF *without* additional legislation as part of dealer licensing regulations.

ATF should promulgate regulations requiring gun dealers to take mandatory steps to secure their inventory to prevent theft. This action can be taken without additional statutory authority.

Require Licensed Gun Manufacturers and Dealers to Perform Background Checks on Their Employees

Although convicted felons and other prohibited persons are barred from possessing or buying guns, there is no requirement that federally licensed gun manufacturers and dealers conduct background checks on employees who sell guns. To make it harder for dangerous people to get guns, prospective gun industry employees should be screened to ensure that they are not prohibited purchasers. Several states already require gun dealers to conduct background checks on employees to ensure that dangerous persons are not selling firearms, and this should be required nationwide.

ATF should promulgate regulations that, as a condition of gun manufacturers and dealer licensing, require licensees to conduct background checks on their employees. This action can be taken without additional statutory authority.

Prevent Dealers from Liquidating Their Inventory Without Background Checks After Their Licenses Have Been Revoked

Even after ATF revokes a dealer's license for violating federal law, it has allowed those dealers to transfer their inventory—frequently hundreds of guns—to their "personal collections," and then sell them. Even worse, former dealers are permitted under federal law to sell guns from their "personal collections" without conducting a Brady background check. ATF can, and should, cease this practice, and it can do so *without* additional legislation.

This "fire sale" loophole was exploited by former NRA [National Rifle Association of Ameria] board member Sandy Abrams, who was cited for more than 900 violations of federal gun laws at his Baltimore gun shop.

Despite Abrams's violations, ATF permitted him to transfer hundreds of guns to his personal collection when his license was revoked. Abrams continued illegally selling guns, and pled guilty in 2008 to selling an assault weapon to a criminal who shot at police officers. Similarly, ATF allowed Ugur "Mike" Yildiz to transfer over 200 guns from the shop's inventory to his personal collection after his license was revoked. Yildiz then illegally sold many of those guns, and many have been linked to violent crimes.

ATF should refuse to allow dealers whose licenses have been revoked from transferring firearms from the store's inventory to their personal collection. This action can be taken without additional statutory authority.

> *"More [gun] regulations limit the deterrent effect of defensive firearms and lead, therefore, to more injuries."*

Laws Controlling Private Gun Ownership Reduce Its Deterrent Effect on Gun Crime

Robert A. Levy

Studies show that laws restricting private gun ownership will not enhance public safety, claims Robert A. Levy in the following viewpoint. Thus, Levy reasons, states and cities that enact gun control laws should bear the burden of proving their effectiveness, which they have yet to do. In fact, he argues, the opposite is true: Gun control laws actually reduce the deterrent effect of guns. Unfortunately, the benefits of the defensive use of guns in the home are not well documented. Levy is chair of the board of directors of the Cato Institute, a libertarian think tank.

As you read, consider the following questions:

1. What two important questions did the *New England Journal of Medicine* and the *Journal of the American Medical Association* articles that Levy addresses raise?

Robert A. Levy, "Doctors for Gun Control," *Regulation*, vol. 31, Winter 2008, pp. 7–9. Copyright © 2008 Cato Institute. All rights reserved. Reproduced by permission.

2. What does Levy claim further complicates correlation studies between suicide rates and gun ownership?

3. What benefit of private gun ownership does the *JAMA* article not consider, according to the author?

Just weeks after the Supreme Court issued its blockbuster opinion in the landmark Second Amendment case *District of Columbia v. Heller*, two prominent medical journals were in print with an editorial and two articles asserting that guns at home are a major public health problem.

One-Sided Coverage

First off the press was the July 31, 2008, *New England Journal of Medicine* [*NEJM*] editorial "Guns and Health," citing statistics from the Centers for Disease Control and Prevention [CDC] on the number of injuries and deaths from handgun use. Five weeks later, the same journal published "Guns and Suicides in the United States," by the Harvard School of Public Health's Matthew Miller and David Hemenway, summarizing studies purporting to establish a direct relationship between suicides and household gun ownership. Four weeks later, Georgetown University law professor Lawrence Gostin expanded on the guns-cause-violence theme in "The Right to Bear Arms," a brief paper on gun control law and politics that appeared in *JAMA: The Journal of the American Medical Association*.

The articles and editorial raise two important questions: Is there persuasive empirical data that lawful gun ownership makes the public less safe? If so, would public safety be enhanced by tighter gun controls? There is a rich academic literature examining those questions, and the literature indicates "No" for both questions.

Disappointingly, neither the *NEJM* nor *JAMA* want to discuss those peer-reviewed studies. Indeed, when I offered to

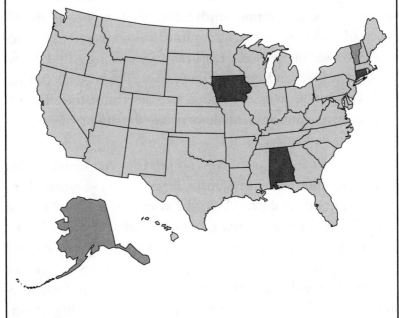

Most States Allow Concealed Weapons

As of 2006, forty states have so-called right-to-carry laws allowing citizens to carry concealed firearms in public. In 36 of the states, "shall issue" laws require the issuance of permits for gun owners who meet standard criteria.

Types of laws

Shall issue

Discretionary issue

No permit

TAKEN FROM: Kenneth Jost, "Gun Violence," *CQ Researcher*, May 25, 2007.

write a short article in response to the *NEJM* editorial, my offer was declined. When I volunteered to convert the short article into an even shorter letter to the editor, that too was declined. Other lawyers have written for the *NEJM*, but none represented Mr. [Dick] Heller before the Supreme Court as I did. Perhaps viewpoint discrimination explains the one-sided coverage of this issue by both the *NEJM* and *JAMA*. So I will share a few of those counterarguments here.

Guns and Safety

The *NEJM*'s editors cite, with justifiable concern, CDC data on handgun-related injuries and deaths. But the editors conveniently ignore a comprehensive 2003 CDC report on the efficacy of firearms and ammunition bans, restrictions on acquisition, waiting periods, registration, licensing, child access prevention laws, and zero tolerance laws. The report's conclusion: There is "insufficient evidence to determine the effectiveness of any of the firearms laws or combinations of laws reviewed on violent outcomes."

"Research has shown," the *NEJM* editorial claims, "that fewer restrictions on handguns will result in a substantial increase in injury and death." To the contrary: a 2004 National Academy of Sciences review of 253 journal articles, 99 books, and 43 government publications evaluating 80 gun control measures concluded that "existing research studies ... do not credibly demonstrate a causal relationship between the ownership of firearms and the causes or prevention of criminal violence or suicide."

The *NEJM* editorial writer does offer one citation to specific data on the relationship between guns and public health: a 1991 *NEJM* article ostensibly documenting a 25 percent decline in gun-related homicides and suicides immediately after the District of Columbia enacted its 1976 gun ban. But that study has been discredited for its biased selection of comparable jurisdictions, failure to adjust for D.C.'s declining population, disregard of other explanatory variables, and selective choice of time periods. Further, a 1996 paper in the *Law & Society Review* found that if the study, which ended in 1987, had been extended by just two years, the observed decline would have disappeared.

Looking at Suicide Data

Interestingly, the District exempted preexisting handguns from its 1976 ban. If handgun availability were positively linked to suicides, one would expect suicides to decline progressively as owners gradually sold, discarded, or removed pre-1976 guns from the city. But the suicide rate was the same in 1998 (7.6 per 100,000) as it was in 1981, and ranged from 4.9 to 11.8 during the intervening period. The decline in suicides reported in the 1991 *NEJM* article was a temporary, random phenomenon.

Looking at suicide data cross-sectionally—e.g., comparing states having the highest rates of gun ownership with states having the lowest rates—Miller and Hemenway conclude in their *NEJM* article that high gun ownership goes hand in hand with high rates of firearm suicide and overall suicide. But numerous studies, not cited in their article, have concluded otherwise. Florida State University criminologist Gary Kleck, for example, cites studies based on local, national, and international data showing that nations with fewer guns do not have fewer suicides. New York University law professor James B. Jacobs confirms that the U.S. suicide rate is equal to the average for industrialized nations, despite America's higher rate of gun ownership.

Correlation studies between suicide rates and gun ownership are further complicated by confounding variables—including differences in the percentages of single-parent households, the portion of the population that hunts, and the preponderance of selected racial and ethnic groups (most importantly, African Americans, who have a much lower suicide rate than whites). The association of confounding variables with both suicide and gun ownership can make it appear that suicide and gun ownership are themselves correlated, when they are not.

Regulation and Safety

Even if it could be shown that suicides, crime, or accidents increase as gun ownership increases, the preventive or remedial effect of gun control must also be demonstrated. On that question, the *NEJM* editorial simply asserts that the problem of firearm injuries "seems certain to be exacerbated with less handgun regulation." That is a gross and careless overstatement. There is little reliable evidence—much less certainty—of a statistically significant inverse relationship between handgun regulations and firearms injuries. In fact, much of the evidence points to a direct relationship: More regulations limit the deterrent effect of defensive firearms and lead, therefore, to more injuries.

Washington, D.C., affords a crystalline example: Since implementation of the District's ban, the city's murder rate has fallen only once below what it was in 1976. The overall violent crime rate in D.C. dropped below its 1976 level in only four years during the three ensuing decades. Most distressing, the District has ranked first or second in yearly murders 15 times since the ban has been in place. FBI [Federal Bureau of Investigation] data for 2006 indicate that the District's murder rate was more than five times higher than the national average, and more than double the rate in comparably sized cities—none of which had gun laws as restrictive as the District's.

Perhaps recognizing that crime data provide compelling support for the proposition that gun control doesn't work, Gostin's article in *JAMA* highlights accident statistics. "A gun in the home is far more likely to be involved in killing a family member than an intruder," insists Gostin. Even if true, the point is irrelevant. The benefit of a gun in the home is not to shoot bad guys; that rarely happens. The real benefit is the deterrent effect on the commission of crime. Peer-reviewed studies indicate that guns are used defensively—almost always brandished, not fired—five times more often than they are involved in violent acts. More important, the *JAMA* article does not consider the countless instances of violent acts *not* under-taken because the potential victims might be able to defend themselves with suitable firearms.

Burden of Proof

One final point: A few seemingly sophisticated statistical analy-ses suggest that more firearms mean more gun violence, and more gun regulations will alleviate the problem. But many more analyses suggest the opposite. How then should a court, considering the trade-off between public health and the Sec-ond Amendment, weigh the evidence? Do the regulators or the firearms rights advocates have the burden of proof? That is a legal, not social science, question.

When courts review regulations to determine whether they pass constitutional muster, judges must first decide how rigor-ously they will scrutinize enactments of the legislative branch. Under so-called rational basis scrutiny, courts typically rubber-stamp whatever the legislature passes as long as the judge can conceive of a legitimate justification for the law. Challengers face a heavy burden in showing that no rational basis exists. At the other extreme is "strict scrutiny," whereby courts will demand proof from government that state interests are com-pelling and the regulation is no more restrictive than neces-sary to attain the desired goal.

In *District of Columbia v. Heller*, the Supreme Court cat-egorically rejected rational basis scrutiny for the review of firearms laws. Something higher is demanded, said Justice An-tonin Scalia, when an express constitutional right is at issue; the District's ban on all functional firearms in the home was unconstitutional "under any of the standards of scrutiny the Court has applied to enumerated constitutional rights." Al-though the Court did not explicitly adopt strict scrutiny, it certainly moved in that direction.

It is clear, post-*Heller*, that government has the burden of proof in justifying gun regulations that might infringe on Second Amendment rights. It is equally clear—notwithstanding the predisposition of the *NEJM* and *JAMA*—that the regulators have not met their burden.

> "Our colleges and universities are safe
> sanctuaries for learning, and we believe
> they would be endangered by the pres-
> ence of concealed handguns."

College Campuses Are Safer
Without Concealed Weapons

Students for Gun Free Schools

*Colleges and universities would be much less safe if students
were able to carry concealed weapons, argues the organization
Students for Gun Free Schools (SGFS) in the following viewpoint. Concealed handguns will not deter rare high-profile campus shooters, SGFS maintains. In fact, the organization reasons,
many of those who carry concealed weapons do not have the
skill needed to help prevent gun crime. Moreover, SGFS asserts,
concealed weapons will only increase the risks that drugs, alcohol, and academic stress create. SGFS was formed in response to
the growing concealed carry on campus movement that followed
the April 2007 shooting at Virginia Tech.*

As you read, consider the following questions:

1. How does the homicide rate at postsecondary institutions compare to the nation as a whole?

"Why Our Campuses Are Safer Without Concealed Handguns," Students for Gun Free
Schools, April 6, 2010. Reproduced by permission.

2. What percentage of full-time college students abuse drugs or drink alcohol on binges at least once a month?

3. Why is it unlikely that campus shooters like those at Virginia Teach and Northern Illinois University would be deterred by the presence of concealed weapons?

In the wake of tragic shootings at Virginia Tech and Northern Illinois University,[1] a group called Students for Concealed Carry on Campus formed to advocate for the "right" of students and faculty to carry concealed handguns at colleges and universities in the United States. This group was quickly joined by the National Rifle Association [of America] and other pro-gun organizations that had been lobbying for years to liberalize America's concealed carry laws.

Safe Places

Frequently lost in the national debate that ensued was the fact that our nation's colleges and universities are some of the safest places in our country in large part because their campuses, in almost all cases, have remained gun-free.

The overwhelming majority of the 4,314 colleges and universities in the United States prohibit students and faculty from carrying concealed handguns on campus (the exceptions include public colleges and universities in Utah; Blue Ridge Community College in Weyers Cave, Virginia; and Colorado State University in Fort Collins, Colorado). Despite high-profile shootings like the ones mentioned above, homicides at American colleges and universities remain rare events.

A 2001 study by the U.S. Department of Education found that the overall homicide rate at postsecondary education institutions was 0.07 per 100,000 of enrollment in 1999. By

---

1. On April 16, 2007, student Seung-Hui Cho shot and killed thirty-two people and wounded many others at Virginia Tech University before killing himself. On February 14, 2008, graduate student Steven Kazmierczak killed five people and wounded many others at Northern Illinois University before killing himself.

comparison, the criminal homicide rate in the United States was 5.7 per 100,000 persons overall in 1999, and 14.1 per 100,000 for persons ages 17 to 29. Another study, conducted by the Department of Justice, found that 93% of violent crimes that victimize college students occur off campus. This research demonstrates conclusively that students on the campuses of postsecondary institutions are significantly safer than both their off-campus counterparts and the nation as a whole.

The Risks of Concealed Handguns

Students for Gun Free Schools (SGFS) believes these results can be attributed largely to strict policies that have kept firearms off our nation's campuses. Our colleges and universities are safe sanctuaries for learning, and we believe they would be endangered by the presence of concealed handguns for the following reasons:

1. Concealed handguns would detract from a healthy learning environment;

2. More guns on campus would create additional risk for students;

3. Shooters would not be deterred by concealed carry permit holders;

4. Concealed carry permit holders are not always "law-abiding" citizens, and

5. Concealed carry permit holders are not required to have law enforcement training.

1) Concealed Handguns Would Detract from a Healthy Learning Environment

In order to foster a healthy learning environment at America's colleges and universities, it is critical that students and faculty feel safe on campus. If concealed carry were allowed on America's campuses, there is no doubt that many students would feel uncomfortable about not knowing whether their professors and/or fellow students were carrying handguns.

Students and teachers must be able to express themselves freely in classroom environments, where discussions frequently touch on controversial topics that arouse passion. The introduction of handguns on our campuses would inhibit this dialogue by creating fear of possible retaliation. Whether it's a classroom debate, a student-teacher conversation about a grade, or an informal interaction in a dormitory; the presence of hidden handguns would restrain the open exchange of ideas that is so critical to the college experience.

Americans, in overwhelming numbers, believe that guns have no place at our colleges and universities. In one national survey, 94% of Americans answered "No" when asked, "Do you think regular citizens should be allowed to bring their guns [onto] college campuses?"

Greater Risk

2) More Guns on Campus Would Create Additional Risk for Students

Allowing concealed carry permit holders to bring handguns onto college campuses would raise a host of public safety concerns for institutions that have a legal duty to provide secure environments for their students, faculty and visitors. As noted in a 2007 report by the Brady Campaign to Prevent Gun Violence, there are four reasons why gun violence would be likely to increase if more guns were present on college campuses: (1) the prevalence of drugs and alcohol; (2) the risk of suicide and mental health issues; (3) the likelihood of gun thefts, and; (4) an increased risk of accidental shootings.

A 2007 study by the National Center on Addiction and Substance Abuse at Columbia University found that "[N]early half of America's 5.4 million full-time college students abuse drugs or drink alcohol on binges at least once a month." Another study found that alcohol is involved in 95% of the violent crime on campus. The combination of alcohol, drugs and guns is a dangerous mix that could lead to additional, and more lethal, violence on campus. A 2002 study by the Harvard School of Public Health compared students who have a firearm at college with those who do not have a firearm. They found that students who have a firearm at college are more likely to binge drink, drive a motor vehicle after binge drinking, use illegal drugs, vandalize property, and get into trouble with the police.

Suicide and mental health are also substantial issues on college campuses. One study found that 24% of college students had thought about attempting suicide and 5% had actually attempted to kill themselves. Firearms, of course, make many types of violence more lethal. Suicide attempts are successful more than 90% of the time when a firearm is used. By comparison, such attempts are fatal only 3% of the time when a drug overdose is the method used. One study that examined college student suicide from 1920–2004 found that, "It is the reduced use of firearms as a method of suicide that is responsible for virtually all of the benefit associated with being a student . . . and that the relationship between student status and firearms may be the key to understanding why students commit suicide at a lower rate than does the general U.S. population."

Allowing concealed handguns on campus would also increase the risk of gun theft and accidental shootings. College dorm rooms are typically small, with few places available to lock up or secure a handgun. They also experience considerable numbers of visitors who could gain unauthorized access to these firearms.

The Deterrence Myth

3) Shooters Would Not Be Deterred by Concealed Carry Permit Holders

The gun lobby frequently advances the argument that shooters target gun-free zones such as college campuses for their attacks because they are unlikely to receive initial resistance.

This ignores the fact that homicides and shootings at American colleges and universities are rare events in large part because of these institutions' current policies regarding firearms on campus. In 2003, for example, there were 11,920 total gun homicides in the United States, but only 10 total murders on the nation's college campuses.

Campus shooters are also frequently suicidal. Most of the campus shootings in America in recent years (i.e., Virginia Tech, Northern Illinois University, Louisiana Technical College, etc.) were murder-suicides. These shooters left home on the morning of their attacks knowing they were going to die by gunfire before the day was over—their goal was simply to take as many people with them as they could. It is unlikely these shooters would have been deterred by the knowledge that their fellow students (or campus faculty) might be armed. In fact, it is possible that a college campus that allows staff and faculty to carry concealed handguns might provide a more attractive target to such shooters. Lacking any fear of death, they might welcome the opportunity to provoke shootouts and cross fire among relatively untrained concealed carry permit holders in order to increase casualties.

There have also been numerous incidents in recent years where shooters have targeted what might be deemed "gun-full zones" for their attacks, including:

May 8, 2006—Michael Kennedy, 18, attacks Fairfax County Police Sully District Station in Virginia, firing more than 70 rounds and killing two officers before police are able to take him down. Kennedy is armed with five handguns and two rifles, including a semiautomatic AK-47 assault rifle, and carries more than 300 rounds of ammunition.

May 19, 2007—Jason Hamilton shoots and kills his wife at home and then attacks a sheriff's department at Latah County Courthouse and a church in Moscow, Idaho. Hamilton kills a total of three people, including a police officer, before taking his own life. He is armed with an AK-47 assault rifle and an M1 carbine despite a long history of domestic violence, mental illness, and run-ins with the police. Local resident and University of Idaho student Pete Hussmann, 20, races to the courthouse on his bike armed with a .45-caliber handgun and is shot four times by Hamilton. "It was like a war zone," says Hussmann. Two other law enforcement officers are wounded.

There is no evidence that suicidal shooters would be deterred from attacks on college campuses by concealed carry permit holders. To the extent that they could provoke firefights with such individuals in crowded college classrooms and create additional mayhem, they might even seek out such confrontations.

Not Always "Law-Abiding" Citizens

4) Concealed Carry Permit Holders Are Not Always "Law-Abiding" Citizens

The gun lobby frequently claims that those with permits to carry concealed handguns are "law-abiding citizens," or even the most law-abiding citizens in their communities. This is not always true.

Two states, Alaska and Vermont, do not even require residents to obtain a permit to carry a concealed weapon. Individuals in these states can buy a handgun through an unregulated private sale (no background check required) and then carry it in public.

38 states have a "shall-issue" policy for concealed carry permits, meaning that officials may not arbitrarily deny an application to those who meet a basic set of requirements. The primary requirement for obtaining a permit in these states is

to pass a background check through the National Instant Criminal Background Check System (NICS). The purpose of the background check is to ascertain whether the applicant is prohibited under federal law from owning and purchasing firearms. Those with felony convictions are automatically prohibited. The only misdemeanor convictions that would prohibit someone from owning and purchasing firearms, however, are those related to incidents of domestic violence. Someone who obtains a concealed carry permit in a shall-issue state could have a rap sheet with other types of misdemeanor convictions, including violent offenses.

The National Instant Criminal Background Check System is also not foolproof. A recent study found that the NICS database is "deeply flawed" and missing millions of disqualifying records. Most troubling, nine out of ten mental health records that would disqualify individuals from purchasing firearms are not currently in the database. One-fourth of felony conviction records have also not been submitted to NICS by the states.

The bottom line is that even if someone passes a background check and qualifies for a concealed carry permit (if their state requires one), that person is not necessarily a law-abiding citizen. They could have a substantial criminal record involving misdemeanor offenses, or a history of mental illness. It is notable that campus shooters including Gang Lu, Wayne Lo, Robert Flores, Biswanath Halder, Seung-Hui Cho, Latina Williams and Steven Kazmierczak passed background checks in acquiring the firearms used in their attacks. Some possessed a concealed carry permit in their home states; others would have qualified had they applied. Finally, individuals who are prohibited under federal law from owning or purchasing firearms can still pass a background check (and potentially qualify for a concealed carry permit) if their disqualifying records have not been transferred to NICS.

Research has demonstrated that those who obtain concealed carry permits can pose a threat to public safety:

Adding Guns to the College Mix

It is difficult to imagine how colleges can provide safe environments if most constituents have the right to carry concealed deadly weapons. Adding guns to the normal conflicts that arise, or to alcohol, drugs, competitive sports, or depression, is a recipe for disaster....

Weapons-related policies can be a significant part of eliminating the risks of violence.

Sandra J. McLelland and Steven D. Frenkil,
"Banning Weapons on Campuses: The Battle Is Far from Won,"
Chronicle of Higher Education, *February 13, 2009.*

A Violence Policy Center study found that Texas concealed handgun license holders were arrested for weapon-related offenses at a rate 81% higher than the general population of Texas aged 21 and older (offenses included 279 assaults, 671 unlawfully carrying a weapon, and 172 deadly conduct/ discharge of a firearm). Between January 1, 1996, and August 31, 2001, Texas concealed handgun license holders were arrested for 5,314 crimes—including murder, rape, kidnapping and theft.

A 2007 investigation by the Florida *Sun-Sentinel* found that the state's permit system had granted concealed carry permits to more than 1,400 individuals who pled guilty or no contest to a felony, 216 individuals with outstanding warrants, 128 individuals with active domestic violence restraining orders, and six registered sex offenders.

Little Training

5) Concealed Carry Permit Holders Are Not Required to Have Law Enforcement Training

The 48 states in the U.S. that allow residents to carry concealed handguns do not require them to have any formal law enforcement training. The training requirement to obtain a concealed carry permit in a "shall-issue" state is typically a day class. Many shall-issue states do not even require the applicant to fire his/her handgun at a range to demonstrate proficiency or even basic competency with the weapon. An example would be Virginia, where a four-hour sit-down session in a classroom is sufficient to meet the state's training requirement.

This is in direct contrast to the intensive training required of law enforcement officers who are currently called on to safeguard our nation's colleges and universities. These officers start receiving training in how to safely handle a sidearm—and in demonstrating discretion in using lethal force—long before they ever see actual duty in their communities. This training then continues throughout their career in law enforcement. Police departments typically require their officers to qualify 1–4 times a year with their duty weapon.

Nonetheless, even trained law enforcement officers rarely hit their targets when firing at other human beings. One 2006 study, examined three decades of bullet hit rates among larger U.S. police departments and found that officers hit their targets approximately 20% of the time. The New York City Police Department's Firearms Discharge Report for 2006 showed similar results. That year, their officers intentionally fired a gun at a person 364 times, hitting their target only 103 times—a success rate of 28.3%. Commenting on that success rate, New York City Police Commissioner Ray Kelly said, "When you factor in all of the other elements that are involved in shooting at an adversary, that's a high hit rate. The adrenaline flow, the movement of the target, the movement of the shooter, the officer, the lighting conditions, the weather . . . I think it is a high rate when you consider all of the variables."

Given the record of trained law enforcement officers, how often would relatively untrained concealed carry permit holders hit their targets when opening fire on college campuses? Recent shootings on America's campuses have occurred in crowded classrooms and involved a great deal of chaos, with students panicked and running for their lives. Concealed carry permit holders discharging their weapons in such situations would be unlikely to have clear lines of fire. If multiple students drew handguns, just identifying the actual "shooter" or target would be challenging. The potential for collateral damage is enormous, even assuming that concealed carry permit holders would make sound decisions about when to discharge their handguns.

Law enforcement officers responding to such emergencies would also face enormous difficulties. If police arrived on the scene of a campus shooting and found multiple students with handguns drawn, how would they know who their target is? This scenario was contemplated by the Virginia Tech Review Panel, which commented: "If numerous people had been rushing around with handguns outside Norris Hall on the morning of April 16 [2007], the possibility of accidental or mistaken shootings would have increased significantly. The campus police said that the probability would have been high that anyone emerging from a classroom at Norris Hall holding a gun would have been shot."

The Self-Defense Myth

Despite the fact that there are more than 200 million firearms in private hands in the United States and 48 states now allow some form of concealed carry, instances in which law-abiding citizens successfully shoot and kill criminals are exceedingly rare. In 2005, there were a total of 12,352 gun-related homicides in the United States. Yet, during the same year, the FBI reported only 143 justifiable homicides involving a firearm. A 2000 study by the Harvard School of Public Health concluded that, "Guns are used to threaten and intimidate far more often than they are used in self-defense. Most self-reported self-defense gun uses may well be illegal and against the interests of society." This is no doubt partially due to the lack of formal training among those purchasing firearms and receiving permits to carry concealed handguns in the United States.

The notion that individuals with concealed carry permits are going to make prudent decisions about when to discharge their firearms on school campuses is dubious at best; as is the notion that these individuals would successfully take down active shooters while avoiding collateral damage in chaotic situations. The safest policy to limit potential violence is to prohibit students and faculty from keeping handguns on campus and allow trained law enforcement officers to provide for campus security.

| *"Current school policies and state laws against concealed carry on campus serve only to stack the odds in favor of dangerous criminals."*

College Campuses Are Less Safe Without Concealed Weapons

Students for Concealed Carry on Campus

The assumption that college campuses are safer because students are not allowed to carry concealed weapons is flawed, argues the organization Students for Concealed Carry on Campus (SCCC) in the following viewpoint. In fact, SCCC claims, none of the feared risks have been realized at the twelve U.S. college campuses that allow concealed weapons. For example, SCCC maintains, no student under the influence of drugs or alcohol has brandished a weapon at these campuses. Students with concealed weapons will, however, be better able to protect themselves from crime, SCCC asserts. SCCC was created in the wake of the April 2007 shooting at Virginia Tech.

As you read, consider the following questions:

1. What is assumed about the presence of guns off campus in the argument that if concealed carry on campus were allowed, students would feel uncomfortable not knowing who had a gun?

2. Why, according to SCCC, is the issue of alcohol consumption and reckless behavior by college students a moot point?

3. Why does SCCC contend that extensive tactical training is not necessary for concealed carry holders?

In response to the unprecedented media attention and public support generated by Students for Concealed Carry on Campus (SCCC), the organization leading the charge to extend concealed carry (of handgun) rights to college campuses, a countermovement has emerged, operating under the banner Students for Gun Free Schools (SGFS). SGFS recently released an essay titled "Why Our Campuses Are Safer Without Concealed Handguns." This attack on the positions of SCCC brings few, if any, new arguments to the table and relies instead on the well-worn arguments put forth by groups like the Brady Campaign to Prevent Gun Violence.

A Leap in Logic

The crux of the SGFS essay is the undeniable fact that college campuses typically have lower crime rates than the cities in which they reside. Tossing academic standards of research and citation to the wind, the essay's introduction simply points out this fact and concludes, "Students for Gun Free Schools (SGFS) believes these results can be attributed largely to strict policies that have kept firearms off our nation's campuses."

Without citing corroborating facts or research, the same gun control advocates who want us to believe that lax gun control laws in nearby states negate the effectiveness of strict gun control laws in the District of Columbia and other tightly regulated cities/states now want us to believe that strict gun control regulations on college campuses are able to stand up against the lax gun control laws in the very cities in which those campuses reside.

To assume a cause-and-effect relationship between the unenforceable gun control regulations on college campuses and the relative safety of college campuses constitutes an astoundingly naïve leap in logic. A similar disparity can be found between the relatively low crime rates in affluent neighborhoods and the higher crime rates in the cities in which those neighborhoods exist. After all, what are college campuses but, essentially, large, affluent neighborhoods?

After making the unsubstantiated claim that strict gun control regulations make college campuses safer, the essay moves on to present five reasons why SGFS believes that allowing concealed carry on college campuses would make colleges less safe:

1. Concealed handguns would detract from a healthy learning environment;

2. More guns on campus would create additional risk for students;

3. Shooters would not be deterred by concealed carry permit holders;

4. Concealed carry permit holders are not always "law-abiding" citizens, and

5. Concealed carry permit holders are not required to have law enforcement training.

The Impact on Intellectual Debate

1) Concealed Handguns Would Not Detract from a Healthy Learning Environment

An opponent of concealed carry on campus isn't doing his or her job unless he or she argues, "Concealed handguns would detract from a healthy learning environment." The SGFS essay contends, "If concealed carry were allowed on America's campuses, there is no doubt that many students would feel uncomfortable about not knowing whether their professors and/or fellow students were carrying handguns." This argument not only ignores the fact that, in the absence of metal detectors and X-ray machines at every campus entrance, students already have no way of knowing who, if anyone, is carrying a gun; it also assumes that students would be made more uncomfortable by the presence of guns on campus than they are by the presence of guns off campus.

In most U.S. states approximately 1% of the population (one person out of 100) is licensed to carry a concealed handgun. Are students afraid to sit in 300-seat movie theaters knowing that, statistically speaking, as many as three of their fellow moviegoers may be legally carrying concealed handguns? Are they afraid to walk through crowded shopping malls knowing that one out of every hundred shoppers they pass is potentially carrying a legally concealed handgun? Or do they go through their daily routines, both on and off campus, never giving much thought to what is concealed beneath the clothing and within the handbags of the people they pass? Does SGFS honestly contend that students on the twelve U.S. college campuses where concealed carry is currently allowed (all ten public colleges in the state of Utah, Colorado State University, and Blue Ridge Community College in Weyers Cave, VA) are afraid to engage in intelligent debate for fear that somebody nearby might have a gun? Does concealed carry discourage debate on the floor of the state legislatures in Texas and Virginia and the other states where it is allowed in the state capitol? . . .

Overblown Concerns

2) More Guns on Campus Would Create Little If Any Additional Risk for Students

The SGFS essay goes on to assert, "More guns on campus would create additional risk for students." Citing a study by the Brady Campaign, the essay points to "(1) the prevalence of drugs and alcohol; (2) the risk of suicide and mental health issues; (3) the likelihood of gun thefts, and; (4) an increased risk of accidental shootings." The essay doesn't mention that after allowing concealed carry on campus for a combined total of one hundred semesters, none of the aforementioned twelve U.S. colleges have seen a single resulting incident of a student under the influence of drugs or alcohol using or brandishing a weapon on campus, a single resulting suicide, a single resulting gun theft, or a single resulting gun accident. . . .

Despite all of these statistics, the issue of alcohol consumption and reckless behavior by college students is a moot point—this is not a debate about keeping guns out of the hands of college students. Allowing concealed carry on college campuses would not change the rules about who can purchase a firearm or who can obtain a concealed handgun license. It also wouldn't change the rules at off-campus parties and bars, the places where individuals over the age of 21 are most likely to consume alcohol. And it would not make it legal to carry a handgun while under the influence of drugs or alcohol. Changing the rules would simply allow the same trained, licensed adults who carry concealed handguns, without incident when not on campus, to do so on campus. There is no reason to assume that the same individuals who aren't getting drunk and shooting people outside of college campuses would suddenly get drunk and start shooting people on college campuses.

SGFS's arguments about suicide and the vulnerability of dorm rooms to theft carry very little weight when viewed in light of the fact that this is not a debate about who can own or carry a gun. The overwhelming majority of suicides are committed in the victim's home. Under current regulations, the only students prohibited from keeping firearms in their homes are students living in on-campus housing. At most colleges, on-campus housing is occupied primarily by freshmen and sophomores, students typically too young to obtain a concealed handgun license. . . .

Concerns about accidental discharges are overblown, to say the least. Accidental discharges of concealed firearms are very rare—particularly because modern firearms are designed with safety in mind and because a handgun's trigger is typically not exposed when it is concealed—and only a small fraction of accidental discharges result in injury. It is silly to suggest that citizens should be denied a right simply because that right is accompanied by a negligible risk.

The Deterrence Effect

3) Shooters May or May Not Be Deterred by Concealed Carry Permit Holders, but Deterring Shooting Sprees Is Only One of Several Potential Benefits

SGFS goes on to argue, "Shooters would not be deterred by concealed carry permit holders." To quote Louisiana State Representative Ernest D. Wooton, speaking at the 2008 SCCC National Conference in Washington, D.C., "If we don't try it, are we going to know?"

Though campus shooters are frequently suicidal, they are not simply suicidal—if they were, they would simply shoot themselves at home and leave everyone else alone. Campus shooters go on armed rampages because they misguidedly seek to make a point or attain infamy. It's hard to attain infamy if a concealed handgun license holder ends your shooting spree before it begins. Even if the knowledge that concealed handgun license holders might be present isn't enough to deter all would-be gunmen, an attempted shooting spree thwarted by a licensee might be enough to deter a few.

The SGFS essay points to two attacks on facilities where the shooters knew that law enforcement officers would be present, as evidence that suicidal gunmen are not deterred by armed resistance. Those particular shooters may not have been deterred, but they also didn't cause nearly as great a loss of life as is often caused by shooters in "gun free zones." In those two incidents, the shooters killed a combined total of five people, less than one-sixth the total body count from the Virginia Tech massacre.

The issue of concealed carry on college campuses is not just about preventing campus shooting sprees. Though it's the mass shootings that get the headlines, college campuses play host to assaults, rapes, and every type of criminal activity found in the rest of society. The question of whether or not concealed carry would deter would-be mass-shooters should not be the determining factor in whether or not it is allowed on college campuses. Why should a 105 lb. woman who is allowed the means to defend herself against a 250 lb. would-be rapist outside of campus not be afforded that same right on campus? Why should a professor who is allowed the means to defend himself at the local bank and at his neighborhood church be forced to hide under his desk listening to gunshots getting closer, with no recourse but to hope and pray the gunman doesn't find him?

Concealed Carry Statistics

4) Concealed Carry Permit Holders Are Not Always "Law-Abiding" Citizens, but They're Statistically More Law-Abiding than Most

Students for Gun Free Schools unnecessarily points out, "Concealed carry permit holders are not always 'law-abiding' citizens." This is true. Likewise, law enforcement officers, elected officials, and clergy members are not always "law-abiding" citizens. Every segment of society has its bad apples, but statistically speaking, concealed carry has fewer than most. Numerous studies by independent researchers and state agencies suggest that concealed handgun license holders are five times less likely than non-license holders to commit violent crimes. A comparison of statistics in the mid-nineties, when Florida was still one of the few shall-issue states, found that Florida concealed handgun license holders were three times less likely to be arrested than were New York City police officers.

Despite the fact that Students for Concealed Carry on Campus does not advocate concealed carry by unlicensed individuals, SGFS finds it necessary to point out that Alaska and Vermont do not require (though Alaska offers) a license to carry a concealed handgun. The essay then goes on to erroneously suggest, "The primary requirement for obtaining a permit in [the 38 shall-issue] states is to pass a background check through the National Instant Criminal Background Check System." In reality, many states, such as Texas, require applicants to submit to extensive state and federal fingerprint and background checks that often take one to three months (far from instant) to complete.

The essay further blurs the line between the requirements to purchase a firearm and the requirements to obtain a concealed handgun license by stating, "The only misdemeanor convictions that would prohibit someone from owning and purchasing firearms, however, are those related to incidents of domestic violence. Someone who obtains a concealed carry permit in a shall-issue state could have a rap sheet with other types of misdemeanor convictions, including violent offenses." The factors that can disqualify an individual from obtaining a concealed handgun license vary from state to state, but most states place certain restrictions and time limits on misdemeanor offenders. For instance, in the state of Texas you cannot obtain a concealed handgun license if you have had any misdemeanor convictions greater than a traffic citation in the past five years. A current license holder who commits a misdemeanor greater than a traffic violation would immediately have his or her license revoked.

The SGFS essay refers to several mass-shooters and erroneously suggests that several of them either possessed or would have qualified for concealed handgun licenses. For example, the essay mentions Seung-Hui Cho, the Virginia Tech shooter, even though his adjudication as a danger to himself and others would have disqualified him from obtaining a concealed handgun license in most shall-issue states. Contrary to the claims of SGFS, mental health rulings are commonly considered by states when deciding whether or not to issue a concealed handgun license. . . .

The truth is that possessing a concealed handgun license and/or having the right to legally carry a firearm does not enable a person to carry a gun or commit a crime. There are no checkpoints where officials screen for guns and check licenses. A person intent on carrying a gun can easily do so throughout modern American society, including on college campuses, regardless of whether or not he or she is licensed to do so. An individual engaged in criminal activity is typically not concerned with the prospect of committing a misdemeanor (carrying a concealed handgun without a license) on his or her way to commit a felony (armed robbery, assault, rape, murder, etc.).

The Truth About Training

5) Concealed Carry Permit Holders Are Not Required to Have Law Enforcement Training Because They're Not Law Enforcement Officers

For its final argument, the essay points out, "Concealed carry permit holders are not required to have law enforcement training." This is true. Concealed carry permit holders are not required to have law enforcement training because they are not law enforcement officers. Law enforcement officers do not go through academy training to learn to carry concealed handguns for self-defense; they go through academy training to learn to be law enforcement officers. Concealed handgun license holders have no need of most of the training received by law enforcement officers. Concealed handgun license holders don't need to know how to drive police cars at high speeds or how to kick down doors or how to conduct traffic stops or how to make arrests or how to use handcuffs. And concealed handgun license holders definitely don't need to spend weeks memorizing radio codes and traffic laws.

Contrary to what SGFS and other opponents of concealed carry might claim, concealed handgun license holders don't need extensive tactical training because they are not charged with protecting the public. Concealed handgun license holders don't go looking for bad guys—it's not their job to act like amateur, one-man SWAT [special weapons and tactics] teams. All a concealed handgun license holder needs to know is how to use his or her concealed handgun to stop an immediate threat of death or serious bodily harm. That type of training *can* be accomplished in the one-day training courses required to obtain a concealed handgun license in most states. . . .

Not surprisingly, the SGFS essay presents the typical far-fetched scenarios of self-defense shootings resulting in "collateral damage" and of multiple students drawing weapons and finding themselves unable to identify the actual "shooter" in prolonged shootouts. This ignores both the findings of a 1997 FBI [Federal Bureau of Investigation] study that concluded that most shootouts last less than ten seconds and the fact that the rate of concealed carry among individuals in their twenties is typically about one-half of one percent. How nine seconds of exchanged gunfire between two armed individuals could possibly lead to greater loss of life than a nine-minute, uncontested execution-style massacre, such as the one that occurred at Virginia Tech, is something Students for Gun Free Schools, like most opponents of concealed carry on campus, doesn't attempt to explain. Likewise, they make no attempt to explain how one of these brief shootouts could lead to multiple students drawing their weapons and losing track of the shooter, when statistically speaking, only about one out of every 200 students would be armed. Given the fact that even a huge 400-seat lecture hall would statistically contain only two students with concealed handgun licenses, the chance of one of those armed students losing track of the actual shooter during a few seconds of exchanged gunfire is highly unlikely.

Saving the Good Guys

Students for Gun Free Schools concludes its essay by suggesting that the relatively small number of justified shooting deaths each year somehow proves that concealed carry is ineffective. Like many opponents of concealed carry, they fail to realize that the key factor is not the number of bad guys killed but, rather, the number of good guys saved. According to a 1991 FBI study, less than one out of a thousand lawful defensive uses of a firearm results in the death of the attacker. By that estimate, firearms are used almost five times more frequently to save lives than to take lives in the U.S.

In the end, Students for Gun Free Schools' arguments against concealed carry on campus, like all arguments against concealed carry on campus, rely entirely on speculation, false assumptions, and emotion. Most college campuses in America are surrounded by neighborhoods where concealed handgun license holders, including college students, lawfully carry concealed handguns at movie theaters, grocery stores, shopping malls, office buildings, restaurants, churches, banks, etc. Yet, we don't hear of spates of accidental discharges or alcohol-fueled shootings by licensees in those places. If the majority of college campuses are safer than their surrounding areas because they don't allow concealed carry on campus, why don't we see higher crime rates at the twelve U.S. colleges that do allow concealed carry on campus? After a combined total of one hundred semesters, why haven't we seen *any* negative results on those twelve campuses? There is absolutely no verifiable evidence to suggest that allowing concealed carry on college campuses makes campuses any less safe; therefore, reason dictates that current school policies and state laws against concealed carry on campus serve only to stack the odds in favor of dangerous criminals who have no regard for school policy or state law. SCCC simply seeks to take the advantage away from those who seek to harm the innocent.

| *"Concealed carry in national parks is a good thing, just like it's a good thing almost everywhere else."*

Laws Allowing Citizens to Carry Concealed Weapons in National Parks Will Make Visitors Safer

Clair Schwan

Law-abiding citizens should be allowed to carry concealed weapons in national parks for self-defense, asserts Clair Schwan, the editor of the Libertarian Logic Web site, in the following viewpoint. Critics of laws allowing concealed carry in national parks fear an increase in poaching, but hunters seldom use concealed weapons, Schwan maintains. Moreover, he argues, laws banning handguns in national parks will not prevent criminals from using them. In fact, Schwan reasons, concealed carry bans make unarmed visitors less safe. The Libertarian Logic Web site supports the free market and promotes individual freedom.

As you read, consider the following questions:

1. What are some of the arguments against carrying concealed weapons in national parks that the author believes are alarmist propaganda?

2. Why does the author believe that allowing concealed carry in national parks is not something cooked up at the end of the Bush administration?

3. What do those who claim concealed weapons pose a "greater risk" in a national park ignore?

After years of discussion, the rules for concealed carry in national parks have been changed for the better. They're just like national forests now—you can carry a weapon for protection.

As a Libertarian, I think with the exception of a correctional institution, concealed carry is a good thing. It allows individuals to have the ability to defend themselves if they so choose.

Prohibition of concealed carry is a prohibition of choice, and a prohibition of self-defense. Both of those prohibitions are wrong.

America is about freedom of choice, and an armed people are a free people. Know arms, know freedom; no arms, no freedom.

Let's first understand the concerns about concealed carry in national parks, then let's examine the facts without all the hysteria.

Concerns About Concealed Carry in National Parks

I'm looking at an editorial opinion from the *Miami Herald* that was reprinted in the *Wyoming Tribune Eagle* under the heading RESTORE THE FIREARMS BAN IN NATIONAL PARKS. It blames the [George W.] Bush administration for caving in to the demands of the NRA [National Rifle Association of America].

It's a lot of general alarmist propaganda, but here are the arguments against national parks concealed carry as near as I can identify them.

- the new rules are harmful

- they do damage

- no one associated with our national parks wanted the gun ban lifted

- most of the respondents during the public comment period opposed lifting the gun ban

- carrying firearms into these national treasures makes no sense

- the weapon ban has worked well all these years

- the concealed carry ban has reduced poaching and kept the level of violence between people to a minimum

- these lands and the people who visit them are now at greater risk

Let's Hear Some Truth and Common Sense

The call to "restore the firearms ban in national parks" is a good example of the uninformed and misguided offering us another heap of steaming, foul-smelling propaganda.

First of all, firearms are not banned from national parks. You can take them into a national park, but they must be unloaded and disabled. The new rules allow concealed carry permit holders to engage in concealed carry in national parks, if they desire to do so.

The editorial opinion talks about visitors now "packing guns" and the fact that there are over 500,000 people in Florida licensed for concealed carry. The writer hopes to conjure up images of 500,000 people roaming around national parks in Florida just looking for a reason to whip out their weapons and start blasting.

The whole issue of allowing concealed carry in national parks isn't something that was cooked up at the end of the Bush administration—it has been in the works for years. It is simply applying age-old rules for national forests to our national parks.

Concealed carry is allowed in national forests, so how is it that national parks should be so different? Each has trees, bushes, animals and visitors—and criminals ready to prey upon animals and visitors.

Apparently the writer believes that handguns (the preferred concealed carry weapon) are ideal for poaching. Clearly the writer isn't a hunter and doesn't know anything about hunting. Only a tiny fraction of hunting is done with any type of weapon that can be considered concealable.

No Safer with Gun Restrictions

The idea that national parks are safe places because of gun restrictions makes about as much sense as saying that Chicago, Los Angeles, New York and Washington, D.C., are safe places because of their firearms restrictions. Yeah right!

The idea that concealed weapons pose a "greater risk" in a national park ignores statistics that clearly show more guns equals less crime and a lower severity of violent crime. There is a clear relationship between places with high violent criminal activity and places with the greatest restrictions on firearms, and often they are one in the same.

Let's remember that laws are for the law abiding. Firearms restrictions don't deter criminals because it isn't their intention to follow laws in the first place. Laws stop criminals about as much as stop signs stop cars.

Firearms restrictions only offer a safer environment for criminals to carry out their activities against the law abiding.

Gun free zones aren't crime free zones—they are only places where criminals have greater confidence of operating among disarmed victims.

Avoiding Disaster

I know of two examples where a single armed man deterred criminal gangs of 3 and 5 members each, simply by showing the criminals approaching the campsite that there would be a price to pay. In each case, the man was camping with his wife in a remote area of a state park, and the campsite intruders approached in a manner that clearly indicated planning for a malevolent intent.

In both of these situations, no police report was made because no crime was committed. So, we have no official record that law-abiding citizens with firearms used them in a legal manner to avoid disaster in a state park.

What difference would it make if the potential victims were camping, fishing or hiking? Aren't they entitled to self-defense from those who would do them harm? Of course they are.

All the opposition to concealed carry in national parks by government officials and the public mirrors similar opposition to concealed carry laws across the country. Our experience shows clearly that violent crime has gone down because responsible citizens have been better prepared to take care of themselves.

In addition, all the predictions of gunfights over traffic accidents and blood in the streets has not materialized. The blood in our streets is still confined mostly to large metro areas where drug deals are common.

Nevertheless, some people cling to the belief that banning concealed carry in national parks has created bliss and reduced crime of all sorts. The truth is simply that criminals will be criminals and they typically don't hang out in national parks, but sometimes they do.

The idea that bans on concealed carry in national parks is responsible for these places being safe is merely an illusion. As for my associates that encountered criminals on the prowl for vulnerable targets in state parks, they know that there is no reason why something like that can't occur in one of our national parks.

Preparing for Self-Defense

If you agree with the *Miami Herald* opinion writer that bans on concealed carry in national parks have "worked well all these years," then I would invite you to imagine yourself back on September 10, 2001, saying that the policies and actions of our intelligence and investigative services have "worked well all these years" protecting Americans. I suppose you'd be right . . . for a little while.

Those who desire to be prepared to defend themselves should be allowed to do so. As Larry Elder so clearly pointed out, gun control proponents "have blood on their hands," and no one knows this better than the criminals and their victims.

Concealed carry in national parks is a good thing, just like it's a good thing almost everywhere else. As a Libertarian, I fight for your freedom, at home, at work, and in our national parks.

> *"Allowing loaded and accessible weapons in our national parks will create a dangerous environment for the millions of Americans and tourists from around the world who visit our national parks every year."*

Allowing Citizens to Carry Concealed Weapons in National Parks Is Dangerous

Dianne Feinstein

Allowing citizens to carry concealed weapons in America's national parks will create a dangerous environment for visitors and wildlife, argues Dianne Feinstein in the following viewpoint. Moreover, Feinstein reasons, lifting the ban in national parks will also be confusing as state concealed carry laws vary and many national parks cross state lines. For these reasons, organizations representing park employees oppose lifting the ban on concealed carry in national parks, she concludes. Feinstein is a Democratic U.S. senator representing California.

As you read, consider the following questions:

1. How does the public rate America's national parks?

Dianne Feinstein, "Allowing Loaded Guns in National Parks a Reckless Move," *San Francisco Chronicle*, December 29, 2008. Reproduced by permission of the author.

2. In Feinstein's opinion, who was the beneficiary of the
   Bush administration's rule change allowing concealed
   carry in national parks?

3. What are the odds of becoming a victim of violent
   crime in the national parks?

With its days numbered, the [George W.] Bush administration has made an unnecessary and dangerous change
to a 25-year-old regulation that bans concealed, loaded firearms in America's national parks and wildlife refuges.

This regulation, created by the [Ronald] Reagan administration, has done an outstanding job of making these special
places among the safest in the nation. And it did so without
imposing unreasonable restrictions on gun owners—it merely
required that weapons be unloaded and kept in a place that's
not readily accessible, such as a car trunk.

An 11th-Hour Change

But this 11th-hour rule change—slipped in by a lame-duck
administration . . . with Congress out of session—will let
people with concealed weapons permits bring loaded firearms
into national parks and wildlife refuges.

This is an astonishingly reckless move, made in the absence of any public outcry in favor of changing this rule. In
fact, the public consistently rates our national parks at the top
of federal government programs that work well. There is no
reason to fix a system that Americans overwhelmingly tell us
is not broken.

Simply put, this is the Bush administration's parting gift to
the gun lobby—at the expense of the health and safety of the
public, park rangers and wildlife.

A Bad Move

Here's why it's a bad move:

Allowing loaded and accessible weapons in our national parks will create a dangerous environment for the millions of Americans and tourists from around the world who visit our national parks every year. These park visitors expect a safe and enjoyable experience—not loaded guns and stray bullets.

Poaching will increase in our national parks, upsetting the delicate balance between park visitors and wildlife.

It will create a confusing patchwork of regulation that will be impossible to enforce. That's because some parks, like Death Valley National Park, cross state lines. California prohibits concealed weapons in its state parks. Nevada does not. Which state's law will apply at Death Valley?

The new regulation itself is vague and confusing because it permits state law on gun possession to determine whether guns are allowed in national parks. But many states—including California—generally allow the carrying of concealed weapons with a permit, but prohibit their possession in state parks. The new regulation isn't clear on which state law applies.

A Sense of Safety

The regulation that the Bush administration repealed goes back more than 100 years in some national parks, including Yellowstone. It was applied across the board in 1983, and it's been critical in giving park visitors a real sense of safety.

This sense is supported by the facts. In fact, the odds of becoming a victim of violent crime in our national parks are 1 in more than 708,000, according to the Coalition of National Park Service Retirees.

That's less than the odds of being struck by lightning.

The people who know our parks best oppose this rule change. They include the retired Park Service employees group; the National Park Rangers Lodge of the Fraternal Order of Police; the National Parks Conservation Association; the Association of National Park Rangers; and the American Hunters and Shooters Association.

These great parks are national treasures, and they should be respected as such.

I agree with what the writer Wallace Stegner said in 1983: "National parks are the best idea we ever had. Absolutely American, absolutely democratic, they reflect us at our best rather than our worst."

If there is any good news, it is this: President-elect Barack Obama will take office on Jan. 20 [2009]. I hope he moves quickly to reverse this monumentally reckless move by his predecessor.[1]

1. Congress passed the bill that repealed the ban on concealed weapons in national parks in the spring of 2009; the rule became effective on February 22, 2010.

Periodical Bibliography

The following articles have been selected to supplement the diverse views presented in this chapter.

E.J. Dionne Jr.	"Beyond the NRA's Absolutism," *Washington Post*, December 10, 2009.
Joanne Ditmer	"How Did Guns in Parks Happen?" *Denver Post*, June 6, 2009.
David Kopel	"Guns in Parks: The Hoplophobes' Travel Guide to the United States," *New Ledger*, May 29, 2009.
Sandra J. McLelland and Steven D. Frenkil	"Banning Weapons on Campuses: The Battle Is Far from Won," *Chronicle of Higher Education*, vol. 55, no. 23, February 13, 2009.
New York Times	"Guns in Parks: Safe, Scary or a Sideshow?" May 22, 2009.
Andrew Potter	"Colleges Can't Be More Like Airports? Why Not?" *Maclean's*, April 30, 2007.
Bill Schneider	"Why the National Park Gun Rule Should Stand," *Crosscut*, January 9, 2009.
John Stossel	"Gun Control Puts People at Risk," *Human Events*, March 10, 2008.
Vin Suprynowicz	"How Many More Will Die in 'Gun-Free' Zones Before the Media Start Asking Why," *Las Vegas Review-Journal*, December 16, 2007.

What Laws and Regulations Should Govern Guns?

Chapter Preface

Federal Bureau of Investigation (FBI) statistics reveal that in nearly 40 percent of murder investigations nationwide, no arrests are made. This statistic, combined with the fact that more than half of all murders are committed with guns, has led advocacy groups such as the Brady Campaign to Prevent Gun Violence to reason that too many murderers with guns remain at large. These advocates suggest that microstamping technology will help law enforcement identify and apprehend some of these armed criminals before they hurt others. Firearm microstamping uses laser technology to engrave a microscopic code number on the firing pin and ejector mechanism of semiautomatic weapons. When the firearm is fired, these etched numbers are transferred to the cartridges, which can be recovered from the crime scene and examined by ballistics experts who can then trace the firearm to its last legal owner. Whether governments should mandate microstamping is a contentious issue. Indeed, one of several controversies in the debate concerning what laws and regulations should govern guns is whether legislation mandating firearm microstamping is necessary to reduce gun violence or an unnecessary restriction based on costly, unproven technology.

Opponents argue that microstamping technology remains untested. Microstamped parts, they maintain, can be easily altered or replaced. Lawrence G. Keane of the National Shooting Sports Foundation asserts that microstamping technology functions unreliably and marks can be easily removed using household tools such as diamond files. Moreover, critics claim, unscrupulous gun owners can easily replace the marked firing pins and ejector mechanism. Microstamping detractors also contend that complying with microstamping mandates will be costly for gun manufacturers. Keane suggests that the estimated cost of implementing this technology could approach as much as $200 per firearm.

Those who support legislation mandating microstamping technology dispute such claims. Joshua Horwitz of the Coalition to Stop Gun Violence maintains that microstamping technology would add only $1 to $6 to manufacturing costs. Moreover, Horwitz asserts, microstamping is not designed to solve all gun crimes. The goal of microstamping mandates, he argues, is to help police deal with crimes such as gang shootings, in which unsophisticated gang members who often use semiautomatic weapons leave shell casings behind at the scene of the crime. Proponents also contend that microstamping will help law enforcement better track firearms from manufacturer to criminals and straw purchasers, those who legally purchase guns for those who could not legally do so, including gang members. According to Connecticut state legislator Andrew J. McDonald, microstamping "is the equivalent of a fingerprint for a gun"[1]

As of this writing, only one state has mandated microstamping. California's microstamping law went into effect January 1, 2010. The implementation of the law has stalled, however, as the patent for the technology remains encumbered. As other states consider mandating microstamping technology, commentators continue to debate the usefulness of this new technology. The authors in the following chapter debate the value of other laws and regulations designed to reduce gun violence. The efficacy of these laws and regulations remains to be seen.

1. Quoted in Gregory B. Hladky, "'Stamping' Would Link Weapon to Crime," *New Haven Register*, March 4, 2008.

> *"The overwhelming majority of legal scholars who have researched the matter conclude that there is a right to arms."*

The Second Amendment Guarantees the Right to Private Gun Ownership

Don B. Kates

Throughout history, Americans have understood the Second Amendment to guarantee an individual right to bear arms, claims Don B. Kates in the following viewpoint. Indeed, he asserts, scholars nationwide, both liberal and conservative, recognize this right. The idea that the Second Amendment does not guarantee such a right is a fiction created by gun control advocates, Kates argues. These arguments, such as the claim that the right can only be exercised in the context of military service, are illogical, he maintains. Kates, a criminologist and civil liberties lawyer, is coauthor with criminologist Gary Kleck of Armed: New Perspectives on Gun Control.

Don B. Kates, "Who's on Second? In a Speech at UCLA, the Author Laws Down the Law," *Handguns*, August–September 2009, pp. 16–18. Copyright © 2009 Intermedia Outdoors, Inc. Reproduced by permission.

As you read, consider the following questions:

1. What other collective rights does Kates claim apply to the individual?

2. Under what conditions are U.S. soldiers issued weapons?

3. What guarantees, according to the author, did James Madison and Thomas Jefferson believe needed correction from the original U.S. Constitution?

I was involved in the 2007 *[District of Columbia v.] Heller* case in which the Supreme Court invalidated Washington, D.C.'s gun bans as contrary to the Second Amendment right to arms. I was recently invited by UCLA's [University of California, Los Angeles's] law school . . . to address the subject. Here's what I told them:

The historical evidence is clear: The Second Amendment was uniformly seen as an individual right by 18th and 19th century Americans. The idea that it was something else is a fiction of the 20th century, invented because even gun-ban advocates realized that the amendment has to mean something.

Gibberish Guised as Theory

The most currently popular inventions are the 'collective rights' view and the new 'sophisticated collective rights' view. The former claims the right to arms belongs to everyone 'collectively' so that no one individual has or can assert it.

A right that everyone has so no one has it? This is not a theory. This is gibberish guised as a theory. It bears emphasis that no collective right advocate has ever bothered explaining what their interpretation of the amendment means or why Congress would write a meaningless 'right' into the Constitution. They have no interest in explaining this gibberish for it was invented just to provide some explanation of the amendment other than an individual right to arms.

Americans Believe the Second Amendment Guarantees Gun Rights

The exact words of the Second Amendment to the Constitution are: "A well regulated Militia, being necessary to the security of a free State, the right of the people to keep and bear Arms, shall not be infringed."

Do you think these words guarantee each person the right to own a gun, or do they protect the right of citizens to form a militia without implying that each individual has the right to own a gun?

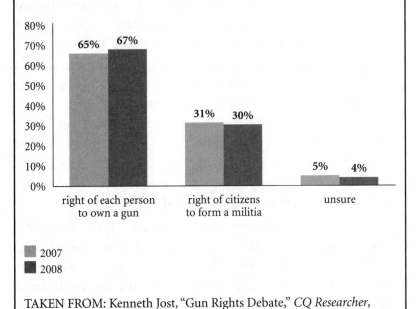

TAKEN FROM: Kenneth Jost, "Gun Rights Debate," *CQ Researcher*, October 31, 2008.

Contrast this 'collective right' gibberish to the 'collective' rights that our Constitution actually does guarantee: The First Amendment protects a 'right of the people' to associate, and for groups to assemble collectively and petition government. That means that any member of a group denied those collective rights may vindicate them by litigating for himself and the group.

Likewise, the 15th and 19th amendments prohibit discrimination against voters because of their race, color or sex.

That means that any person denied the right to vote because of membership in a group defined by race, color or sex may sue to vindicate her own right and those of the other group members. The 'collective right' view of the Second Amendment is an oxymoron which clashes with the way every other collective right works.

The Militia Context Problem

The 'sophisticated collective right' theory is even worse. It posits a right to arms that can only be exercised 'in the context of' militia or military service. Since its proponents have not adduced even one example of what that means, let me suggest some. Imagine a good old boy from down South enlists. He started hunting when he was eight and by 18 is a superb marksman. So the Army makes him a cook and gives him a stove instead of a rifle. If he has a right to arms 'in the context of military service,' does that mean he can sue the Army and a court will order the military to give him a rifle and reassign him as an infantryman? Of course it doesn't!

Under current military practice, soldiers serve unarmed. On base they don't have either their own arms or military arms. When committed to a combat zone, they are issued particular weapons which the Army deems suitable to duties it assigns them. Soldiers do not get to possess personal arms. Any soldier fool enough to demand his 'right to arms in the context of military service' would end his military career in the stockade.

For instance, to the dismay of experienced shooters, the arms the military issues today are far less powerful than those soldiers had 60 years ago when General [George S.] Patton declared the M1 rifle the finest instrument of war ever devised for infantry. Does anyone here think there is a 'right to arms in the context of military service' so soldiers can demand the Army issue them old M1s rather than puny new M16s? (Incidentally, when the CIA [Central Intelligence Agency] hires mercenaries it gives them M16s; but as soon as they kill an insurgent they pick up his AK-47 and throw away the M16.)

If it does not mean any of these things, what does it mean to call the Second Amendment a right to arms that can (only) be exercised 'in the context of' militia or military service? And why do these queries have to be raised by an opponent of the collective right theories?

Inventing Meaning

Why have the theories' proponents not detailed what those theories mean? Those theories are just gibberish frantically dreamed up to invent some meaning for the Second Amendment other than what it means.

An older anti-gun invention claims the amendment was intended to restore state control over the militias. This is not gibberish. It is an intelligible theory. But it is clearly wrong. Here are some of the major historical problems:

1. The amendment uses the phrase 'right of the people,' which everywhere else in the Constitution denotes individual rights; the amendment does not use words like 'powers' or 'authority,' which is how government powers are described everywhere else throughout the Constitution;

2. The Second Amendment was not the product of some devotee of states' rights and powers vis-à-vis [in regard to] the federal government. It was authored by James Madison who was so extreme an advocate of federal power vis-à-vis the states that he deemed the Constitutional Convention a failure because it rejected his proposal for a federal veto power over all state legislation.

3. Madison and his mentor [Thomas] Jefferson did not see the federal powers in the original Constitution as exces-

sive vis-à-vis the states; if anything needed correction, they believed, it was the lack of a set of guarantees for personal rights, not a lack of guarantees for states' rights;

4. Madison expressly told Congress that his Bill of Rights guaranteed personal rights to individuals and had nothing to do with state powers;

5. Far from thinking the Second Amendment would meet their desires, the Anti-Federalists (the advocates of restoring state powers over the militia) in the First Congress sought to accomplish it by separate proposed constitutional amendments—which were defeated by the Federalist-majority Senate;

6. Neither in Congress nor the state legislatures was there either any objection to an individual right clause or any suggestion that it would restore state power over the militia; the only objections made were to the militia clause on the ground that it did not do anything;

7. The amendment follows early state constitutional rights provisions in having a prefatory clause (the militia clause) preceding the rights declaration; the principle of construction then as now was that the prefatory clause cannot narrow or nullify the declared right; and

8. Far from the Second Amendment preserving state powers over the militia, from the earliest time the Supreme Court has consistently held federal authority over the militia to be plenary with state authority limited to matters as to which the federal government has not spoken.

Since 1980 almost 200 law review articles have discussed the Second Amendment. Upwards of 175 of those 200 endorse the individual right to arms. The authors include leading scholars. While some are conservatives like Eugene Volokh, they also include outstanding liberals like Bill Van Alstyne, Leonard Levy, Sandy Levinson, Scot Powe and Alan Dershowitz.

In sum, the overwhelming majority of legal scholars who have researched the matter conclude that there is a right to arms—even though many of them wish there were not.

2

> "Five [U.S. Supreme Court] justices re-
> wrote the Second Amendment to en-
> shrine their policy views about restric-
> tive gun laws."

Judicial Activism Wrongly Established a Second Amendment Right to Private Gun Ownership

Dennis A. Henigan

In the U.S. Supreme Court decision District of Columbia v.
Heller, *the majority justices abused their role to press their own
ideological views, asserts Dennis A. Henigan in the following
viewpoint. Justice Antonin Scalia took the "keep and bear Arms"
language of the amendment out of context, Henigan maintains.
As a result, he claims,* Heller *creates a right to use guns "in defense of hearth and home" when nothing in the text of the Second Amendment grants this right. Henigan is vice president for
law and policy at the Brady Center to Prevent Gun Violence.*

As you read, consider the following questions:

1. How will historians regard *Heller*, in Henigan's view?

Dennis A. Henigan, "The *Heller* Paradox: A Response to Robert Levy," *CATO Unbound*,
July 16, 2008. Copyright © 2008 Cato Institute. All rights reserved. Reproduced by permission.

2. What unusual step did the majority justices take?

3. According to the author, what strategy is key to the National Rifle Association's attempt at making gun control an attack on personal possession of guns?

I appreciate the opportunity to participate in this [*Cato Unbound*] discussion. It also gives me a chance to congratulate [attorney] Bob Levy and his team publicly on their historic victory in *District of Columbia v. Heller.*

Heller as Judicial Activism

Levy's discussion of judicial activism opens the door to a discussion of the merits of the majority opinion. I can't resist walking through it. My view is that legal historians will regard the *Heller* decision as a prototypical misuse of judicial power to advance an ideological agenda. Not *Bush v. Gore* [the Supreme Court decision that decided the result of the 2000 presidential race between George W. Bush and Al Gore], but close.

Levy defines judicial activism as "rendering legal judgments based on the judge's public policy preferences." "Results-oriented jurisprudence, based on subjective value judgments," he writes, "may be proper for a legislator, but not for a judge." This is a dead-on description of Justice [Antonin] Scalia's opinion, in which five justices rewrote the Second Amendment to enshrine their policy views about restrictive gun laws. Conservative law professor Douglas Kmiec agrees. In an extraordinary recent article disclosing his own family's gun violence tragedy, Kmiec praises Justice Scalia's "career of reminding his fellow judges how important it is not to read their own personal experiences or desires into the law," but finds that principle dishonored in Scalia's *Heller* opinion. "From their high bench on that morning," he wrote, "it would not be the democratic choice that mattered, but theirs. Constitutional text, history, and precedent all set aside."

The "results-oriented jurisprudence" of the majority is most evident in its treatment of the constitutional text. In *Heller*, Justice Scalia's textualism is transparently inconsistent and manipulative. In opposition to the "militia purpose" view of the Second Amendment, he advances numerous examples of the usages of the phrases "keep Arms" and "bear Arms" to refer to a non-militia right. For example, he cites a 1734 text providing, "Yet a Person might keep Arms in his House, or on his Estate, on the Account of Hunting, Navigation, Travelling, and on the Score of Selling them in the way of Trade or Commerce, or such Arms as accrued to him by way of Inheritance." How does he know this usage of "keep Arms" is unrelated to militia service? Because the context suggests that it refers to private activities alone. As to "bear Arms," he cites various state constitutional provisions that guarantee "every citizen a right to bear Arms in defence of himself and the State." We know "bear Arms" includes a non-militia right in those provisions because of the context in which the phrase appears, particularly the phrase "defence of himself." These examples demonstrate that *context is critical to meaning*.

A Phrase Ripped Out of Context

When it comes to the Second Amendment, however, Scalia interprets "keep and bear Arms" by ripping the phrase out of context; that is, by artificially separating the phrase from its stated purpose of ensuring a "well regulated Militia . . . necessary to the security of a free State." The issue is not whether "keep Arms" and "bear Arms" could have non-militia meanings in other contexts. The issue is the meaning of the phrase "keep and bear Arms" in the context of a provision declaring the importance of a "well regulated Militia . . . to the security of a free State." The closest contemporary usage of "the right of the people to keep and bear Arms" was in the Massachusetts Bill of Rights, which provided that "the people have a right to keep and bear arms for the common defense," in a provision that also warned of the dangers of peacetime armies and urged civilian control of the military. How do we know that "keep and bear arms" in that provision did not refer to individual self-defense? Because its context says otherwise. In a similar way, the meaning of the same phrase in the Second Amendment is affected by the context supplied by the militia language. Only through highly selective reliance on context to derive meaning does Scalia arrive at his predetermined conclusion.

The majority disguises its unprincipled use of context through the sleight of hand of referring to the militia language as "prefatory" as opposed to the other "operative" language of the amendment. It treats the militia language as if it were equivalent to "whereas" clauses in legislative language, but this is clearly wrong. The preamble to the Constitution may be analogous to legislative "whereas" clauses, in that it is not independently enforceable as a source of substantive powers or rights. But the first thirteen words of the Second Amendment are only less "operative" than the remainder because five justices of the Supreme Court have now decreed it to be so.

Justice Scalia's tortured path thus "elevates above all other interests the right of responsible citizens to use arms in defense of hearth and home," in a text in which this interest is entirely hidden and in which the "security of a free State," not the security of "hearth and home" is the only expressed purpose of the guarantee. Grotesque. (To borrow a word from Justice Scalia).

The Legal Implications

As indefensible as the majority's opinion is in addressing the meaning of the Second Amendment, it nevertheless is likely to have a limited practical effect on gun laws less restrictive than a handgun ban. In this, the *Heller* decision should prove to be a sharp disappointment to the gun lobby and other Second Amendment extremists.

First, it is clear that there are not five votes on the Supreme Court for applying a "strict scrutiny" standard to gun laws. This was an important setback for [Dick] Heller [one of the plaintiffs in the case who challenged Washington, D.C.'s handgun ban] and a great victory for public safety.

Second, the majority took the highly unusual step of commenting on the constitutionality of numerous laws not at issue in the case, making it clear that a wide range of gun control laws remain "presumptively lawful." These include (1) prohibitions on carrying concealed weapons (which the Court found were held lawful under early state Second Amendment analogues); (2) prohibitions on firearms possession by felons and the mentally ill; (3) laws forbidding firearms in "sensitive places" like schools and government buildings; (4) laws imposing "conditions and qualifications" on the commercial sale of arms (which could include background checks, waiting periods, licensing, etc.); (5) bans on "dangerous and unusual weapons" (which could include machine guns and assault weapons); and (6) laws regulating the storage of firearms to prevent accidents. Then, in a telling footnote, the Court adds that its list of "presumptively lawful regulatory measures . . . does not purport to be exhaustive."

Although we will no doubt see an avalanche of Second Amendment claims (most by criminal defense lawyers on behalf of their clients seeking to avoid indictments and convictions for violations of gun laws), generally the lower courts are likely to interpret *Heller* as giving a constitutional green light to virtually every gun control law short of a handgun ban. Regardless of whether the *Heller* majority's newly discovered right eventually is incorporated as a restraint on the states, its significance may well prove more symbol than substance.

The Political Implications

Levy's discussion of next steps on the political front focuses on the short-term questions for the District of Columbia and on the two presidential candidates. He misses the true long-term political significance of *Heller*.

One of the gun lobby's core arguments against reasonable gun laws is that every new restriction on guns is but a step down the "slippery slope" to gun confiscation and thus is a threat to ordinary gun owners. The "slippery slope" is key to the National Rifle Association's [NRA's] strategy to make the gun issue a "cultural" or "wedge" issue politically. It frames gun control as an attack on a valued personal possession and, indeed, on a way of life symbolized by that possession.

In short, the gun lobby needs the debate to be about banning guns that are commonly used by law-abiding Americans. By erecting a constitutional barrier to a broad gun ban, the *Heller* ruling may have flattened the gun lobby's "slippery slope," making it harder for the NRA to use fear tactics to motivate gun owners to give their time, money and votes in opposing sensible gun laws and the candidates who support those laws. This is especially true since the majority of gun owners support reasonable gun control proposals on their merits. A recent poll shows that 83% of gun owners support closing the "gun show loophole" by extending Brady [Brady Handgun Violence Prevention Act] background checks to private sales at gun shows. Conversely, the ruling may make it easier for advocates of stronger gun laws to ensure that gun control is viewed as the public safety issue that it is, rather than as a divisive, cultural issue.

This is the *Heller* paradox. A conservative majority violated every concept of judicial restraint to create a new constitutional right that may have little practical impact on gun control laws, but may instead weaken the gun lobby's power to block the sensible gun control proposals that will dominate the debate in the future. Viewing *Heller* from the perspective of the NRA's leadership, an old expression comes to mind: "Be careful what you wish for. It could come true."

> "By closing the gun show loophole and enhancing enforcement, the federal government can dramatically reduce the criminal activity at gun shows that ... threatens public safety."

Gun Show Loopholes Should Be Closed

City of New York

According to the City of New York in the following viewpoint, law enforcement has long known that gang members, criminals, and gun traffickers buy guns illegally at gun shows. In this excerpt from a study conducted by the City of New York, the author claims that private sellers can sell firearms at gun shows without a background check. Moreover, the city argues, at gun shows prohibited buyers can purchase guns through straw purchases, in which someone other than the buyer fills out the required paperwork. Based on its study, the city recommends closing the gun show loopholes and more rigorously enforcing existing gun laws.

As you read, consider the following questions:

1. Why are gun shows a unique marketplace for guns?

2. For what two questions did the City of New York undercover investigation seek answers?

3. How, according to the report, can Congress assist the ATF in its effort to enforce existing laws?

Every weekend, thousands of Americans in all parts of the country attend local gun shows. Organized by gun-owners associations or professional promoters, the shows offer a chance to browse among dozens, and sometimes hundreds, of vendors. For many Americans, gun shows are a family outing. For the gun enthusiast, there are a huge variety of guns—new and used long guns and handguns, historical curios or related accessories—and for the general shopper there are often other vendors selling clothing, books, or local crafts. The vast majority of vendors and customers at gun shows are law-abiding citizens out to enjoy a day with others who share a common interest.

Unfortunately, gun shows are also considered a significant source of guns used in crimes. According to ATF [Bureau of Alcohol, Tobacco, Firearms and Explosives], 30 percent of guns involved in federal illegal gun-trafficking investigations are connected in some way to gun shows. In response to these concerns, the City of New York launched an undercover investigation of illegal sales at seven gun shows across three states. The investigation shows it is both feasible and easy for criminals to illegally buy guns at gun shows.

A Unique Marketplace

Gun shows are a unique marketplace for guns because they feature sales from two types of vendors—federal firearm licensees (FFLs) and private sellers. By law, FFLs include anyone who sells guns professionally—at a gun store, a pawnshop, from their home, or at a gun show. Private sellers are individuals who are not "engaged in the business" but who may make "occasional sales" from their "personal collection." FFLs and private sellers are subject to different federal standards regarding gun sales, most importantly regarding background checks and record keeping. FFLs are required to check every buyer in the National Instant Criminal Background Check System (NICS) to prevent sales to felons, domestic violence misdemeanants or other federal categories of prohibited purchasers. NICS checks are done over the phone and are generally instantaneous. FFLs are also required to maintain the paperwork that connects each gun sold to its buyer. These requirements are designed to keep guns out of the hands of prohibited purchasers and prevent gun trafficking by allowing law enforcement to trace guns recovered in crime to their original point of sale.

The Gun Show Loophole

In contrast, because private sellers are presumed to be occasional sellers or hobbyists, they are under minimal regulation. They are not required to run background checks or keep records of their gun sales. However, even though federal law exempts private sales from background checks, it is still a felony for private sellers to sell to an individual they "know" or "have reason to believe" is a prohibited purchaser. Private sellers' exemption from background checks and record keeping is often referred to as the "gun show loophole." Even though this exemption applies regardless of where private sales take place, gun shows form a central market for prohibited purchasers to connect with private sellers who make anonymous gun sales.

Federal law enforcement agencies have repeatedly expressed concerns about the impact of the gun show loophole on crime. According to a 1999 report by the Justice and Treasury Departments, "gun shows leave a major loophole in the regulation of firearms sales" because they "provide a large market where criminals can shop for firearms anonymously." ATF has said "[gun] shows provide a ready supply of firearms to prohibited persons, gangs, violent criminals, and illegal firearms traffickers." Presidents Bill Clinton, George W. Bush, and Barack Obama have all called for the end of private sales without instant background checks at gun shows.

Gun Show Crimes

In addition to concerns about private sales at gun shows, ATF has noted that even FFLs who sell firearms at gun shows are a source of illegally trafficked guns. In 1999, the Departments of Justice and Treasury and ATF reported that 34 percent of the investigations connected to gun shows involved licensed dealers. According to ATF's report, FFLs at gun shows committed numerous federal crimes, including selling to out-of-state residents, selling without a background check, and engaging in straw purchases. A straw purchase—a federal felony—occurs when a dealer allows someone to fill out the paperwork and undergo the background check, but that person is not the actual buyer of the gun.

With no records of private sales at gun shows, it is almost impossible to know the exact extent of criminal activity that occurs there. In fact, there are no definitive answers to many basic questions one might ask about gun shows: the number of gun shows in America; how many guns are sold at gun shows; or how many private sellers operate at gun shows. The very aspects of gun shows that make them attractive to criminals—the lack of background checks and record keeping— also make it impossible to gather comprehensive information about undocumented sales that occur at those shows.

An Undercover Investigation

To shed light on the practices of firearms sellers at gun shows, the City of New York launched an undercover investigation of illegal sales. The investigation covered seven gun shows spread across three states: Nevada, Ohio, and Tennessee. Working un-

Where Crime Guns Come From

Licensed retailers are the leading *initial* source of crime guns. Of persons incarcerated for serious crimes involving guns, as many as 19% purchased their guns personally from a retail store or pawnshop. Others employ surrogate or "straw" purchasers to buy guns from licensed retailers on their behalf. But far and away, the leading *proximate* source of crime guns is the private sales market. More than 85% of recovered crime guns have gone through at least one private party transaction following their initial sale by a licensed retailer.

Garen Wintemute, Inside Gun Shows: What Goes on When Everybody Thinks Nobody's Watching: Executive Summary, Violence Prevention Research Program, Department of Emergency Medicine, University of California, Davis, School of Medicine, 2009.

dercover, agents conducted "integrity tests" of 47 sellers—both licensed dealers and private sellers—by simulating illegal gun sales at gun shows.

The investigation sought answers to two questions:

1. Question 1: Would private sellers sell guns to people who said they probably could not pass a background check?

2. Question 2: Would licensed dealers sell guns to people who appear to be straw purchasers?

The Results

- 63 percent of private sellers approached by investigators failed the integrity test by selling to a purchaser who said he probably could not pass a background check; some private sellers failed this test multiple times at multiple shows.

- 94 percent of licensed dealers approached by investigators failed the integrity test by selling to apparent straw purchasers.

- In total, 35 out of 47 sellers approached by investigators completed sales to people who appeared to be criminals or straw purchasers.

Investigators also observed that some private sellers appeared to be illegally "engaged in the business" of selling firearms without a license, including a seller who sold to investigators at three different shows and who acknowledged selling 348 assault rifles in just under one year—for approximately $174,000 in revenue.

Proposed Solutions

Gun shows are popular weekend attractions. But additional steps can be taken by Congress and federal law enforcement to both preserve gun shows as a place to legally buy and sell guns and help prevent illegal sales to criminals and gun traffickers.

- *Close the gun show loophole.* Federal law should require background checks and records for all sales by private sellers at gun shows.

- *Increase enforcement of existing laws.* ATF should increase its enforcement efforts at gun shows by regularly conducting integrity tests of licensed and private sellers, investigating private sellers engaged in the business of selling guns without a license, and identifying whether recovered crime guns were purchased at gun shows. Congress should assist these efforts by providing additional resources to ATF.

By closing the gun show loophole and enhancing enforcement, the federal government can dramatically reduce the criminal activity at gun shows that arms criminals and threatens public safety.

> *"Proposals [to restrict gun show sales] would simply create a bureaucratic nightmare—shutting down the shows while leaving criminal markets untouched."*

Background Checks at Gun Shows Are Unnecessary

National Rifle Association-Institute for Legislative Action

To control gun show sales, anti-gun organizations have manufactured false claims about gun shows, argues the National Rifle Association-Institute for Legislative Action (NRA-ILA) in the following viewpoint. Few criminals buy their guns at guns shows, the author maintains. In addition, the NRA-ILA argues, some of the guns that anti-gun organizations claim are purchased by terrorists at gun shows are not even available at these shows. Regulating gun show sales would not reduce gun violence, the NRA-ILA asserts; regulation would simply create unnecessary bureaucracy for legitimate gun sales. NRA-ILA is an organization that lobbies for limited gun control legislation.

As you read, consider the following questions:

1. What happens to people who "engage in the business" of selling guns without a license?

2. What did a 2001 Bureau of Justice Statistics study find?

3. What, according to the viewpoint, does a glance at TV or newspaper coverage of the Middle East show?

Gun shows are large, public events that for many decades have been held in convention centers and banquet halls, attended by gun enthusiasts, hunters, target shooters, law enforcement and military personnel, and their families. Under federal law, firearm dealers—persons engaged in the business of selling firearms for profit on a regular basis—are required to conduct background checks on anyone to whom they sell any firearm, regardless of where the sale takes place. Federal law also provides that a person who is not a dealer may sell a firearm from his personal collection without conducting a check.

Though Congress specifically has applied the background check requirement to dealers only, and specifically exempted from the dealer licensing requirement persons who occasionally sell guns from their personal collections, gun prohibition activists call this a "loophole." Gun prohibitionists also falsely claim that many criminals get guns from gun shows; the most recent federal study puts the figure at only 0.7 percent.

After many months of claiming they wanted a bill that required sales of guns at gun shows, by non-dealers, to be subject to the background check requirement, anti-gun members of Congress voted against such a bill, because it did not contain other provisions designed to put gun shows out of business. Some of the most relevant facts in the debate over gun show legislation include:

The Myth of "Unlicensed Dealers"

Under current federal law, it is illegal to "engage in the business" of "dealing in firearms" without a license from the Bureau of Alcohol, Tobacco, Firearms and Explosives. "Engaged in the business" means buying and selling firearms as a regular business with the objective of profit. Violations carry a five-year prison sentence and a $250,000 fine.

A licensed dealer may do business temporarily at a gun show, just as he could at his permanent licensed premises. Every legal requirement applies equally at both types of location, including background checks and record keeping on all transactions.

People who "engage in the business" without a license can be arrested and convicted of a federal felony—whether they "engage in business" at a gun show, or out of a home, office, or vehicle.

Gun Shows Are Not a Source of "Crime Guns"

A 2006 FBI [Federal Bureau of Investigation] study of criminals who attacked law enforcement officers found that within their sample, "None of the [attackers'] rifles, shotguns, or handguns . . . were obtained from gun shows or related activities." Ninety-seven percent of guns in the study were obtained illegally, and the assailants interviewed had nothing but contempt for gun laws. As one offender put it, "[T]he 8,000 new gun laws would have made absolutely [no difference], whatsoever, about me getting a gun. . . . I never went into a gun store or to a gun show or to a pawnshop or anyplace else where firearms are legally bought and sold."

A Bureau of Justice Statistics (BJS) report on "Firearms Use by Offenders" found that fewer than 1% of U.S. "crime guns" came from gun shows, with repeat offenders even less likely than first-timers to buy guns from any retail source.

This 2001 study was based on interviews with 18,000 state prison inmates and is the largest such study ever conducted by the government.

Previous federal studies have found few criminals using gun shows. A 2000 BJS study, "Federal Firearms Offenders, 1992–98," found only 1.7% of federal prison inmates obtained their gun from a gun show. Similarly, a 1997 National Institute of Justice study reported less than 2% of criminals' guns come from gun shows.

Gun Shows and Terrorism

Anti-gun organizations have tried to claim that terrorists buy guns at gun shows. Yet the cases they point to don't prove their point.

One suspect followed to gun shows was later found "unloading shipments of automatic weapons, explosives, grenades and rocket launchers" in Beirut. These arms, of course, are not available at U.S. gun shows.

Another gun buyer "was arrested in an investigation of the September 11 attacks." But the probe never linked him to the attacks, and there was no indication that he ever shipped guns overseas.

Another case involved an Irish man convicted for using a "straw buyer" at a Florida show to purchase guns from a licensed dealer, for shipment back to Ireland. But in this case, the system worked—the smuggler was convicted and sentenced to four years in prison.

A glance at any TV or newspaper coverage of the Middle East shows that terrorists have no shortage of access to firearms, and far more powerful weapons, without resorting to highly regulated markets in the United States.

Gun Show Legislation Overreaches

Many legislators have proposed to restrict gun show sales, but their proposals would simply create a bureaucratic nightmare—shutting down the shows while leaving criminal mar-

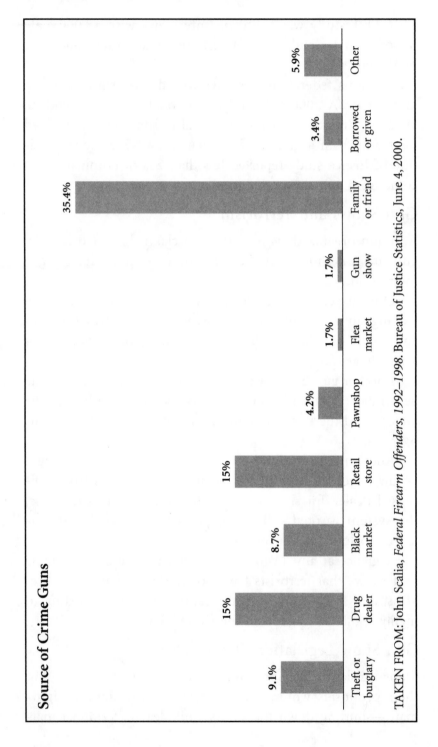

Source of Crime Guns

TAKEN FROM: John Scalia, *Federal Firearm Offenders, 1992–1998*. Bureau of Justice Statistics, June 4, 2000.

kets untouched. Among other problems, various gun show bills (such as H.R. 96 in the 110th Congress)[1] would:

- *Create gun owner registration.* "Special firearms event operators" would have to submit names of all "vendors" to the U.S. Justice Department both before and after the show—whether or not any of the vendors sold a gun. A private citizen who enters a gun show hoping to sell or trade a firearm, but who does not find a buyer and leaves with his own gun, would be on file with the Justice Department forever as a "special firearms event vendor."

- *Require registration of gun shows.* This bureaucratic requirement would allow an anti-gun administration to harass event organizers for paperwork violations. It would also allow government agents to harass gun owners who gather for purposes other than selling guns.

- *Allow harassment of show organizers and vendors.* H.R. 96, for instance, allows inspection, at a gun show, of a show promoter's or dealer's entire business records—including records of transactions that occurred at other shows or at a dealer's licensed place of business. These inspections are time consuming for licensees and highly intrusive; conducting business at a gun show while simultaneously undergoing a compliance inspection would be impossible.

- *Turn casual conversations into "gun show sales."* A person could still agree to sell a gun to a neighbor in a conversation over the backyard fence; but if the same conversation took place at a gun show, the background check requirement would forever apply to that gun. This unworkable and unenforceable system would even

---

1. H.R. 96 never became law.

apply to a gun that a seller and buyer talk about at a gun show, but don't have with them.

- *Fail to provide for true instant checks.* The biggest controversy during the 1999 debate on gun show legislation was how long a "delay period" should be allowed for investigation of a questionable background check. The Lautenberg Amendment allowed three business days—the same as current law for dealers at their regular places of business. That delay would, of course, be impractical for a weekend gun show.

> "How many more innocent Americans must die before federal lawmakers return to their senses and restore the assault-weapons ban?"

The Assault Weapons Ban Should Be Reinstated

Delaware County Daily Times

In the following viewpoint, the editors of the Delaware County Daily Times *argue that the federal government should reinstate the assault weapons ban to prevent tragedies such as the April 2009 murder of three Pittsburgh, Pennsylvania, police officers. Keeping military-style weapons out of the hands of U.S. civilians poses no threat to hunters, the authors assert. Moreover, the Second Amendment did not guarantee the right of Americans to wound or kill numerous fellow citizens in mere seconds, the editors reason. In fact, they maintain, law enforcement personnel nationwide applauded the original ban. The* Times *serves the Delaware County, Pennsylvania, community.*

As you read, consider the following questions:

1. What, according to the authors, motivated U.S. Senator Dianne Feinstein to champion the federal assault weapons ban?

2. What happened to the federal assault weapons ban in 2004?

3. What does the viewpoint contend would be hard for gun advocates to disprove about the cliché "Guns don't kill people, people kill people"?

Fifteen years ago, members of Congress enacted one of the most sensible pieces of legislation in the history of U.S. government.

They passed the federal assault-weapons ban. They didn't deprive Americans of guns. They didn't even force them to undergo waiting periods before buying them.

They simply made it illegal for civilians to purchase 19 named firearms with two or more "military-style features" including the Russian AK-47 assault rifle and the Israeli Uzi. They limited gun owners to ammunition magazines of no more than 10 bullets.

The 1994 legislation was championed by U.S. Sen. Dianne Feinstein, D-Calif., who was appalled by the 1984 shooting rampage at the McDonald's restaurant in San Diego that left 21 dead, and by the shooting deaths of five people several years later in a Stockton elementary school yard. The legislation seemed like a win-win situation.

People who kept guns for security purposes or for hunting still had weapons at their disposal while reduced accessibility to weapons designed for combat made Americans in general less vulnerable to mass attack.

Circumventing the Law

Some unscrupulous gun manufacturers found ways to circumvent the law by marketing attachments that converted compliant weapons into non-compliant ones. One of them was used 10 years ago today [April 20, 1999] by the two students responsible for the Columbine High School shooting rampage in Colorado that ended in the deaths of 13 students, one teacher and the teenaged gunmen themselves.

The Columbine massacre was a grim reminder of just how important it is to keep military weapons out of the hands of civilians. The federal assault-weapons ban was applauded by many, especially by law enforcement officials nationwide.

But, despite their pleas, federal legislators allowed the ban to expire in 2004. And so, the carnage has continued.

The most horrific incident occurred on April 16, 2007, when senior English major Seung-Hui Cho killed 32 students and faculty members before turning the gun on himself at Virginia Polytechnic Institute [and State University, or Virginia Tech] in Blacksburg. It was the deadliest shooting rampage in U.S. history.

Cho had a history of mental illness and clearly that should have been caught in a background check before he was allowed to purchase a 9 mm Glock 19 pistol and a box of ammunition in March 2007 from a Roanoke, Va., firearms store. However, if the federal assault-weapons ban had still been intact, Cho would not have been able to legally purchase a gun with a high-capacity magazine. The Glock has a capacity of 15 rounds with magazines available for up to 33 rounds.

Last week, [Pennsylvania] Gov. Ed Rendell urged Congress to reenact the federal assault-weapons ban. A longtime advocate of gun control, Rendell was especially motivated by the April 4 deaths of three Pittsburgh police officers who, while responding to a domestic disturbance call, were allegedly shot by a 22-year-old man wielding an AK-47.

"Time and time again, across the length and breadth of our great country, our police are finding themselves outgunned," said Rendell.

Assault Weapons and Crime

The 2003 Violence Policy Center study *"Officer Down"—Assault Weapons and the War on Law Enforcement* revealed that from 1998 through 2001, one in five law enforcement officers slain in the line of duty was killed with an assault weapon. Such high-profile events are in addition to the countless incidents that occur almost daily in which assault weapons are used in robberies, assaults on police officers, and shootings that do not result in the headlines generated by a mass killing. One recent example from March 23, 2004: A six-year-old Richmond, Virginia, girl was shot in the head and chest with bullets fired from an AK-47 after gunfire erupted during an argument between two groups of men in a parking lot.

Violence Policy Center,
"A Further Examination of Data Contained
in the Study On Target *Regarding Effects of*
the 1994 Federal Assault Weapons Ban," April 2004.

Prospects for reenactment of the assault-weapons ban look slim if a letter written last month to U.S. Attorney General Eric Holder is any indication. Sixty-five House Democrats, five of them Pennsylvanians, indicated they would oppose reenacting the ban.

Answering Assault-Weapons Ban Critics

Other than pleasing weapons manufacturers and gun-toting constituents, there can be no logical reason for their opposition. Cries that the ban would be unconstitutional ring hollow. Our Founding Fathers didn't have in mind weapons that could mow down innocent citizens in a matter of seconds when they wrote the Second Amendment. Such high-powered weapons did not exist in the Revolutionary War era of militias.

The claim that criminals will acquire assault weapons no matter what the law doesn't nullify the value of banning them.

It only stands to reason that the more guns in circulation, the more there are available to those who obtain them illegally through straw purchases and theft.

And while gun advocates are fond of invoking the cliché, "Guns don't kill people, people kill people," they would be hard-pressed to prove that guns, especially assault weapons, don't make it easier.

Delaware County residents experienced firsthand the consequences of assault weapons on Oct. 30, 1985, when Sylvia Seegrist opened fire with a Ruger .22-caliber semiautomatic rifle at Springfield Mall, killing three and seriously injuring six shoppers. She had purchased the military-style weapon for $104 from Best Products in Marple in March 1985.

But members of Congress need not remember that far back to understand the danger of assault weapons in the hands of civilians. In the last six weeks, 44 people have died in the United States due to rampages by gunmen. The largest carnage occurred on April 4 when a registered gun owner with permits for two semiautomatic rifles opened fire at a Binghamton, N.Y., immigration services center, killing 13 people and then himself.

How many more innocent Americans must die before federal lawmakers return to their senses and restore the assault-weapons ban?

> "A legislatively mandated post–[assault weapons ban] study found that the ban had no discernible effect on crime rates."

The Assault Weapons Ban Should Not Be Reinstated

Steven Warrick

The 1994 federal assault weapons ban did not significantly reduce crime and should not be reinstated, argues Steven Warrick in the following viewpoint. Arguments that reinstituting the ban would reduce gun violence in Mexico are flawed and unfair, he claims. Moreover, he reasons, Americans should not have to sacrifice their rights to eliminate Mexico's gun violence problem. Warrick periodically writes on gun issues for the Daily Utah Chronicle, *an independent student newspaper serving the University of Utah community in Salt Lake City.*

As you read, consider the following questions:

1. What, according to the author, is the main thing that differentiates banned assault weapons from other weapons?

Steven Warrick, "Reinstating Automatic Weapon Ban Would Be Ineffective," *Daily Utah Chronicle*, April 10, 2009. Reproduced by permission.

2. What does the author contend every sovereign nation decides for itself?

3. To what does the author compare the effect of a U.S. assault weapons ban on the drug violence in Mexico?

American gun control advocates are seeking to use the bloody Mexican drug war as an excuse to institute a new ban on semiautomatic assault weapons. This would be a major mistake for two reasons. First, it would represent a sacrifice of the constitutional rights of Americans for the problems of another nation. Second, a renewed semiautomatic assault weapons ban would do little to disarm the Mexican drug cartels.

An Ineffective Ban

The "Federal Assault Weapons Ban [AWB]," which prohibited the sale of semiautomatic versions of certain military-style weapons to civilians, was part of a 1994 crime bill. Americans, however, have had semiautomatic assault weapons for many years, including a number designed by Utah's own John M. Browning a century ago. The main thing that differentiated the banned weapons was their appearance. As many predicted, a legislatively mandated post-AWB study found that the ban had no discernible effect on crime rates.

Notwithstanding the ban's ineffectiveness, gun control advocates have been trying to bring the AWB back ever since its expiration in 2004. So far, they have failed, but Mexico's drug war has given them a new rationale to justify reviving the AWB.

The conflict in Mexico between the cartels for control of access to the lucrative American drug market has been truly horrific. According to Mexican journalist Maria de la Luz González, some 10,475 people died in this conflict from December 2006, when Mexican President Felipe Calderón took office, through March 2009.

Misplaced Blame

Many, including Calderón, the American media and gun control advocates, have attempted to lay part of the blame on ' American gun laws. Mexico has some of the strictest gun control laws on earth, yet a large number of weapons are smuggled in from other places, including the United States, where firearms ownership is protected by the Second Amendment.

At a news conference on Feb. 25, 2009, Attorney General Eric Holder responded to a reporter's question with, "Well, as President [Barack] Obama indicated during the campaign, there are just a few gun-related changes that we would like to make, and among them would be to reinstitute the ban on the sale of assault weapons. I think that will have a positive impact in Mexico, at a minimum."

Holder's statement was met with a hail of criticism, including remarks from Utah Reps. Jim Matheson and Rob Bishop, who are members of a task force on gun rights. Other anti-gun politicians like Hillary Clinton and Sen. John Kerry have persisted on this track, despite the criticism Holder endured.

Terrible as the situation in Mexico is, Americans should not have to surrender their constitutional rights. People like Joseph Stalin have proven that it is possible to drastically reduce crime with sufficiently draconian measures. We could largely eliminate our drug problem by giving the police the authority to order drug tests of anybody, without probable cause and sentence all those found to be in violation to 30 years of solitary confinement. But this is not the kind of society most Americans would want to live in. Each sovereign nation decides for itself what balance of liberty and order it wants to live with.

Looking for Other Explanations

Mexico abolished the death penalty Dec. 9, 2005, which might have played a role in the nation's increase in crime. Americans have decided the right to self-defense, enshrined in the Second Amendment, is important enough to risk the possibility that criminals might have easier access to guns.

At the same time, a new AWB in the United States would do little, if anything, to deprive the cartels of weapons. There have been, for example, some 100 million AK-47-type rifles made, and they are still in production, including at a new factory in Venezuela. These are widely available throughout the world, as are some of the other items the cartels use, such as grenades and antitank weapons (which are not available on the American civilian market).

The cartels have the means to smuggle weapons in and some international arms merchants, like pizza parlors, will deliver if the order is large enough.

A new AWB in the United States will have about as much effect on drug violence in Mexico as stopping beer sales in one store will have on fraternity drinking.

Periodical Bibliography

The following articles have been selected to supplement the diverse views presented in this chapter.

Jimmy Carter — "What Happened to the Ban on Assault Weapons?" *New York Times*, April 27, 2009.

Philip J. Cook, Jens Ludwig, and Adam M. Samaha — "Gun Control After *Heller*: Threats and Sideshows from a Social Welfare Perspective," *UCLA Law Review*, 2009.

David Hogberg — "To *Heller* and Back," *American Spectator*, May 2009.

Mark A. Keefe IV — "The Truth About Gun Shows," National Rifle Association-Institute for Legislative Action (NRA-ILA), October 1, 2009. www.nraila.org.

Jim Kessler — "Deepen Gun Ownership," *Democracy*, Spring 2008.

Los Angeles Times — "Targeting Gun Shows," October 16, 2009.

Penni Mitchell — "The Big Guns," *Herizons*, Winter 2010.

New York Times — "Gun Crazy in the Senate," July 21, 2009.

Supreme Court Debates — "Does the Second Amendment Apply to All U.S. Citizens?" 2010.

Tara Wall — "Right to Carry?" *Washington Times*, July 1, 2008.

For Further Discussion

Chapter 1

1. Tom Diaz claims that U.S. guns fuel Mexican drug-war violence. William P. Hoar argues that gun control advocates exaggerate the number of U.S. guns used in Mexican drug wars to promote stricter gun control laws. To support his claim, Hoar attacks the interpretation of Mexican drug-war gun statistics by gun control activists. Do you think attacking Mexican drug-war gun statistics is sufficient to prove that the majority of Mexican drug-war guns come from places other than the United States? Explain why or why not.

2. Matthew Miller and David Hemenway assert that gun ownership increases the risk of suicide. Don B. Kates disagrees. The authors of both viewpoints cite different types of evidence to support their claims. Which type of evidence do you find more persuasive? Explain.

3. Marian Wright Edelman maintains that the United States has the morally alarming distinction of having the highest rate of child gun deaths in the developing world. The National Rifle Association-Institute for Legislative Action (NRA-ILA) claims that gun safety education is effective to reduce fatal gun accidents among children. Do you think the NRA-ILA's education program is adequate to address the child gun deaths that Edelman laments in her viewpoint? Why or why not?

4. The authors of the viewpoints in this chapter have a variety of different affiliations that might influence their views on the seriousness of the gun violence problem. Which author's affiliation do you think has the most significant

impact on the author's rhetoric and which has the least? Which do you think is most persuasive?

Chapter 2

1. Bob Herbert asserts that the ready availability of guns in the United States explains the nation's gun violence problem. John R. Lott Jr. argues that reducing the availability of guns by banning them simply puts guns in the hands of criminals. Both authors cite facts and statistics to support their claims. Do the facts and statistics each author submits in support of his claim defeat the opposing view? Explain why or why not?

2. Dariusz Dziewanski claims that pop culture images often associate guns with success and power among marginalized young people. This association, he argues, contributes to the problem of gun violence. Andrew Stephen argues that American culture itself promotes gun violence. Do you agree? What role do you think cultural images play in gun violence?

3. Of the various factors that the authors in this chapter claim contribute to gun violence, which factor do you think plays the greatest role and which the least significant role? Explain.

Chapter 3

1. The Brady Campaign to Prevent Gun Violence asserts that laws controlling private gun ownership reduce gun crime. Robert A. Levy counters that the opposite is true—gun control actually reduces the deterrent effect of gun ownership. Which viewpoint do you find more persuasive?

2. How is the rhetoric of Students for Gun Free Schools and Students for Concealed Carry on Campus similar to that of the Brady Campaign to Prevent Gun Violence and Robert A. Levy? How do their arguments differ from these

authors respectively? Does the uniqueness of the college
campus environment inform your analysis? Explain.

3. Dianne Feinstein and Clair Schwan hold opposing views
concerning the carrying of concealed weapons in national
parks. Feinstein believes that the carrying of concealed
weapons in national parks is dangerous, while Schwan
believes that concealed weapons will protect law-abiding
gun owners. Which viewpoint do you find more persuasive? Does the uniqueness of national parks inform your
analysis? How does this differ from your analysis of the
college campus environment, if at all?

Chapter 4

1. Don B. Kates argues that the U.S. Supreme Court decision
in *District of Columbia v. Heller* finally validated the Second Amendment right of individuals to own and possess
arms. Dennis A. Henigan argues that the decision was an
abuse of judicial authority—that nothing in the Second
Amendment grants an individual right to arms. If both
authors cite scholars and legal authority to support their
views, what differences in the viewpoints persuade you to
accept one point of view over the other?

2. The City of New York claims that background checks at
gun shows are necessary to prevent guns from getting into
the hands of criminals. The National Rifle Association-
Institute for Legislative Action argues that background
checks are unnecessary. What rhetorical strategy does each
use to support its claim? Which do you find more persuasive?

3. The editors of the *Delaware County Daily Times* argue
that the Second Amendment was not intended to grant
the right to assault weapons. Reinstating the ban on these
weapons, they claim, would help prevent tragic mass murders. Steven Warrick disagrees. He asserts that the ban was
lifted because it did not reduce crime. The authors of

these viewpoints cite different evidence and use dissimilar rhetoric. Which evidence and rhetorical style do you believe is more persuasive?

Organizations to Contact

The editors have compiled the following list of organizations concerned with the issues debated in this book. The descriptions are derived from materials provided by the organizations. All have publications or information available for interested readers. The list was compiled on the date of publication of the present volume; the information provided here may change. Be aware that many organizations take several weeks or longer to respond to inquiries, so allow as much time as possible.

American Bar Association (ABA)

Special Committee on Gun Violence, 740 Fifteenth Street NW
Washington, DC   20005-1019
e-mail: jarrattk@staff.abanet.org
Web site: www.abanet.org/gunviol/home.html

Since 1965 the American Bar Association (ABA) has sought to address the problem of gun violence and to inform policy regarding the regulation of firearms. Over the decades, the ABA has addressed the issue in the context of an overall strategy to combat violent crime and is in support of a more closely regulated gun trade. The ABA also believes that the nation's culture of violence is the result of many societal factors such as racial intolerance, poverty, out-of-wedlock births, divorce, widespread alcohol and drug abuse, the prevalence of child abuse and neglect, the failure of educational institutions, and the glorification of violence in movies and other media. The association publishes the *ABA Journal* and specialty journals including *Criminal Justice*, recent issues of and excerpts from which are available on its Web site.

American Civil Liberties Union (ACLU)

125 Broad Street, 18th Floor, New York, NY   10004-2400
(212) 549-2500

e-mail: aclu@aclu.org
Web site: www.aclu.org

The American Civil Liberties Union (ACLU) champions the rights set forth in the U.S. Constitution and the Bill of Rights. The union interprets the Second Amendment as a guarantee to form militias, not as a guarantee of the individual right to own and bear firearms. The ACLU believes that gun control is constitutional and necessary. The ACLU publishes the semi-annual *Civil Liberties* in addition to policy statements and reports, many of which are available on its Web site.

Brady Campaign to Prevent Gun Violence and Brady Center to Prevent Gun Violence
1225 Eye Street NW, Suite 1100, Washington, DC   20005
(202) 898-0792 (Campaign); (202) 289-7319 (Center)
fax: (202) 371-9615 (Campaign); (202) 408-1851 (Center)
Web sites: www.bradycampaign.org; www.bradycenter.com

The primary goal of both the Brady Campaign to Prevent Gun Violence and the Brady Center to Prevent Gun Violence is to create an America free from gun violence. Through grass-roots activism, both organizations work to reform the gun industry, educate the public about gun violence, and develop sensible regulations to reduce gun violence. The organizations publish facts sheets, issue briefs, and special reports on their Web sites, including "Kids and Guns in America" and "Domestic Violence and Guns."

Cato Institute
1000 Massachusetts Avenue NW
Washington, DC   20001-5403
(202) 842-0200 • fax: (202) 842-3490
Web site: www.cato.org

The Cato Institute is a libertarian public policy research foundation. It evaluates government policies and offers reform proposals and commentary on its Web site. Its publications include articles such as "Fighting Back: Crime, Self-Defense, and the Right to Carry a Handgun" and "Trust the People: The Case Against Gun Control." It also publishes the magazine *Regulation*, the *Cato Policy Report*, and books such as *The Samurai, the Mountie, and the Cowboy: Should America Adopt the Gun Controls of Other Democracies?*

Citizens Committee for the Right to Keep and Bear Arms (CCRKBA)

Liberty Plaza, 12500 Northeast Tenth Place
Bellevue, WA 98005
(425) 454-4911 • fax: (425) 451-3959
e-mail: InformationRequest@ccrkba.org
Web site: www.ccrkba.org

The Citizens Committee for the Right to Keep and Bear Arms (CCRKBA) believes that the U.S. Constitution's Second Amendment guarantees and protects the right of individual Americans to own guns. It works to educate the public concerning this right and to lobby legislators to prevent the passage of gun control laws. The committee is affiliated with the Second Amendment Foundation and has more than six hundred thousand members. It publishes several magazines, including *Gun Week*, *Women & Guns*, and *Gun News Digest*. News releases, fact sheets, editorial columns from *Women & Guns*, and "Hindsight" editorials from *Gun Week* are available on its Web site.

Coalition for Gun Control

PO Box 90062, 1488 Queen Street W
Toronto, Ontario M6K 3K3
    Canada
(416) 604-0209 • fax: (416) 604-0209
e-mail: 71417.763@compuserve.com
Web site: www.guncontrol.ca

The Coalition for Gun Control was founded in the wake of the 1989 Montreal massacre in which a misogynist with a Ruger Mini-14 and a large-capacity magazine shot twenty-eight people at l'École Polytechnique, killing fourteen young female engineering students. The Canadian organization formed to reduce gun death, injury, and crime. It supports strict safe storage requirements, possession permits, a complete ban on assault weapons, and tougher restrictions on handguns. The coalition publishes press releases and backgrounders. Its Web site provides information on firearms death and injury, illegal gun trafficking, and Canada's gun control laws.

Coalition to Stop Gun Violence (CSGV)
1424 L Street NW, Suite 2-1, Washington, DC   20005
(202) 408-0061
e-mail: csgv@csgv.org
Web site: www.csgv.org

The Coalition to Stop Gun Violence (CSGV) lobbies at the local, state, and federal levels to ban the sale of handguns to individuals and to institute licensing and registration of all firearms. It also litigates cases against firearms makers. Its publications include various informational sheets on gun violence and the *Annual Citizens' Conference to Stop Gun Violence Briefing Book*, a compendium of gun control fact sheets, arguments, and resources. On its Web site, CSGV publishes articles on assault weapons, gun laws, and other gun violence issues.

Gun Owners of America (GOA)
8001 Forbes Place, Suite 102, Springfield, VA   22151
(703) 321-8585 • fax: (703) 321-8408
e-mail: goamail@gunowners.org
www.gunowners.org

Gun Owners of America (GOA) is a nonprofit lobbying organization that defends the Second Amendment rights of gun owners. It has developed a network of attorneys to help fight court battles to protect gun owner rights. GOA also works with members of Congress, state legislators, and local citizens to protect gun ranges and local gun clubs from closure by the government. On its Web site, GOA publishes fact sheets and links to articles including "People Don't Stop Killers, People with Guns Do" and "Is Arming Teachers the Solution to School Shootings?"

Independence Institute

13952 Denver West Parkway, Suite 400, Lakewood, CO   80401
(303) 279-6536 • fax: (303) 279-4176
e-mail: amy@i2i.org
Web site: www.i2i.org

The Independence Institute supports gun ownership as both a civil liberty and a constitutional right. Its Web site contains articles, fact sheets, and commentary from a variety of sources, including "Making Schools Safe for Criminals," "Is Gun Control a New Religion?" and "Kids and Guns: The Politics of Panic."

Jews for the Preservation of Firearms Ownership (JPFO)

PO Box 270143, Hartford, WI   53027
(262) 673-9745 • fax: (262) 673-9746
e-mail: jpfo@jpfo.org
Web site: www.jpfo.org

Jews for the Preservation of Firearms Ownership (JPFO) is an educational organization that believes Jewish law mandates self-defense. Its primary goal is the elimination of the idea that gun control is a socially useful public policy in any country. On its Web site, JPFO provides links to firearms commentary.

National Crime Prevention Council (NCPC)

2345 Crystal Drive, Suite 500, Arlington, VA   22202-4801
(202) 466-6272 • fax: (202) 296-1356
Web site: www.ncpc.org

The National Crime Prevention Council (NCPC) is a branch of the U.S. Department of Justice. Through its programs and educational materials, the council works to teach Americans how to reduce crime and to address its causes. It provides readers with information on gun control and gun violence. The NCPC's publications include the newsletter *Catalyst*, which is published ten times a year, and articles, brochures, and fact sheets, many of which are available on its Web site.

National Rifle Association of America (NRA)

11250 Waples Mill Road, Fairfax, VA   22030
(703) 267-1000 • fax: (703) 267-3989
Web site: www.nra.org

With nearly 3 million members, the National Rifle Association of America (NRA) is America's largest organization of gun owners. It is also the primary lobbying group for those who oppose gun control laws. The NRA believes that such laws violate the U.S. Constitution and do nothing to reduce crime. In addition to its monthly magazines *America's 1st Freedom, American Rifleman, American Hunter, InSights,* and *Shooting Sports USA,* the NRA publishes numerous books, bibliographies, reports, and pamphlets on gun ownership, gun safety, and gun control, some of which are available on its Web site.

Second Amendment Foundation (SAF)

12500 Northeast Tenth Place, Bellevue, WA   98005
(425) 454-7012 • fax: (425) 451-3959
Web site: www.saf.org

A sister organization to the Citizens Committee for the Right to Keep and Bear Arms, the Second Amendment Foundation (SAF) is dedicated to informing Americans about their constitutional right to keep and bear firearms. It believes that gun control laws violate this right. The foundation publishes numerous books including *Armed: New Perspectives on Gun Control; CCW: Carrying Concealed Weapons;* and *The Concealed Handgun Manual: How to Choose, Carry, and Shoot a Gun in Self Defense.* Reports, articles, and commentary on gun issues are available on its Web site.

U.S. Department of Justice, Office of Justice Programs

810 Seventh Street NW, Washington, DC   20531
Web site: www.ojp.usdoj.gov

The U.S. Department of Justice (DOJ) strives to protect citizens by maintaining effective law enforcement, crime prevention, crime detection, and prosecution and rehabilitation of offenders. Through its Office of Justice Programs, the department operates the National Institute of Justice, the Office of Juvenile Justice and Delinquency Prevention, and the Bureau of Justice Statistics. The Bureau of Justice Statistics provides research on crime and criminal justice. The offices of the DOJ publish a variety of crime-related documents on their respective Web sites.

Violence Policy Center (VPC)

1730 Rhode Island Avenue NW, Suite 1014
Washington, DC   20036
(202) 822-8200 • fax: (202) 822-8205
Web site: www.vpc.org

The Violence Policy Center (VPC) is an educational foundation that conducts research on firearms violence. It works to educate the public concerning the dangers of guns and supports gun control measures. The VPC's publications include *Drive-By America*; *A Shrinking Minority: The Continuing Decline of Gun Ownership in America*; and *When Men Murder Women: An Analysis of 2005 Homicide Data*. The center's Web site also includes fact sheets, press releases, and studies on concealed carry laws, assault weapons, and other firearms violence issues.

Bibliography of Books

Amnesty International | *The Impact of Guns on Women's Lives.* Oxford, England: Oxfam International, 2005.

Joan Burbick | *Gun Show Nation: Gun Culture and American Democracy.* New York: New Press, 2006.

Robert H. Churchill | *To Shake Their Guns in the Tyrant's Face: Libertarian Political Violence and the Origins of the Militia Movement.* Ann Arbor, MI: University of Michigan Press, 2009.

Philip J. Cook and Jens Ludwig | *The Social Costs of Gun Ownership.* Cambridge, MA: National Bureau of Economic Research, 2004.

Saul Cornell | *A Well-Regulated Militia: The Founding Fathers and the Origins of Gun Control in America.* New York: Oxford University Press, 2006.

Wendy Cukier | *The Global Gun Epidemic: From Saturday Night Specials to AK-47s.* Westport, CT: Praeger Security International, 2006.

Barna William Donovan | *Blood, Guns, and Testosterone: Action Films, Audiences, and a Thirst for Violence.* Lanham, MD: Scarecrow Press, 2010.

Arnold Grossman | *One Nation Under Guns: An Essay on an American Epidemic.* Golden, CO: Fulcrum, 2006.

Bernard E. Harcourt
Language of the Gun: Youth, Crime, and Public Policy. Chicago, IL: University of Chicago Press, 2006.

David Hemenway
Private Guns, Public Health. Ann Arbor, MI: University of Michigan Press, 2004.

Douglas Kellner
Guys and Guns Amok: Domestic Terrorism and School Shootings from the Oklahoma City Bombing to the Virginia Tech Massacre. Boulder, CO: Paradigm, 2008.

Caitlin Kelly
Blown Away: American Women and Guns. New York: Pocket Books, 2004.

Gary Kleck
Point Blank: Guns and Violence in America. New Brunswick, NJ: Aldine Transaction, 2005.

Abigail A. Kohn
Shooters: Myths and Realities of America's Gun Cultures. New York: Oxford University Press, 2004.

Wayne LaPierre
Guns, Freedom, and Terrorism. Nashville, TN: WND Books, 2003.

John R. Lott Jr.
The Bias Against Guns: Why Almost Everything You've Heard About Gun Control Is Wrong. Washington, DC: Regnery, 2003.

Jeffrey D. Monroe
Homicide and Gun Control: The Brady Handgun Violence Prevention Act and Homicide Rates. New York: LFB Scholarly, 2008.

Robert J. Spitzer   *The Politics of Gun Control.* Washington, DC: CQ Press, 2008.

Charles Fruehling Springwood, ed.   *Open Fire: Understanding Global Gun Cultures.* New York: Berg, 2007.

Irvin Waller   *Less Law, More Order: The Truth About Reducing Crime.* Westport, CT: Praeger, 2006.

Franklin E. Zimring   *The Great American Crime Decline.* New York: Oxford University Press, 2007.

Index

A

Abortion provider murder, 110–111

Advocates for gun control. *See* Gun control advocates/advocacy

al Qaeda terrorist attack (9/11/2001), 28, 90

Alcohol, Tobacco, Firearms and Explosives (ATF) Bureau, 42–43, 141–145

Allen, Matt, 53

American Hunters and Shooters Associations, 187

American Journal of Psychiatry, 129

American Legion, 77

Armed: New Perspectives on Gun Control (Kates), 66

Armed Career Criminal Act (1984), 16

Army recruitment station attack, 111–112

Arulanandam, Andrew, 22, 83

Assassinations, 15, 136

Assault weapons
ban efforts, non-reinstatement of, 226–229
ban efforts, reinstatement of, 221–225
banned sale of, 17, 51, 72, 138
choice for mass murders, 111
"cop-killing" handguns, 47
ease of legal sale of, 41, 45, 82–83, 95–96, 225
Holder's ban support, 54, 141, 224, 228
Mexico's use of, 54
Obama's ban efforts, 55
in Pittsburgh police murders, 105
See also Brady Law; Military-style weapons

Association of National Park Rangers, 187

Availability of guns
Brady Campaign data, 88
Constitution on, 14
hate groups and, 114
mental illness and, 128
reduced violence data, 90–93
suicide risks from, 57–68, 151
U.S. imports, 54
in the U.S., 33
violence increased by, 85–88
Virginia Tech shooting and, 129–130
See also Gun shows

B

Background checks, 97, 161
ATF opinion, 145–146
Bush/Obama support for, 210
current federal law, 95
gun show loophole, 72, 96, 207
Holder's support of, 138–140
mental illness and, 84
NRA opposition, 94, 96
opposition to gun show loophole, 212
record limitations, 140
Seung-Hui Cho experience, 82–83, 223

in shall-issue states, 174
support for gun show loophole, 214–220
types of firearms, 49
unlicensed sellers, 114, 139
See also Brady Law; National
Instant Criminal Background
Check System
Banning of weapons
crimes increased by, 93
in Great Britain, 93
Holder's support of, 54, 141,
224, 228
murder rates and, 91–92
non-reinstatement of efforts,
226–229
Obama's efforts, 55
reinstatement of efforts, 221–
225
sales prevention, 17, 51, 72,
138
suicide and, 32
"Banning Weapons on Campuses:
The Battle Is Far From Won"
(Frankil/McLelland), 163
Barnett, Paul, 82
Berman, Douglas, 135
The Bias Against Guns (Lott, Jr.),
90
Bill of Rights (U.S. Constitution),
38–39
Blair Holt Act (Blair Holt's Fire-
arm Licensing and Record of
Sale Act of 2009), 55
Bloomberg, Michael, 70
Borinsky, Mark, 15–16
Brady Campaign to Prevent Gun
Violence, 27, 83, 136–146
See also Helmke, Paul
Brady Center to Prevent Gun Vio-
lence, 19, 134

Brady Handgun Violence Prevention Act, 107
Brady Law (Brady Handgun Violence Prevention Act)
background check require-
ments, 47–48, 107, 112, 205
children/teenage violence data,
86
college campus report, 158,
171
concealed-carry law success,
34
description, 45–46
firearm numbers data, 87
gun violence reduction stance,
136–146
Helmke's presidency of, 83
homicide by ethnicity data,
100
intrastate sales and, 48
licensed dealer requirement,
47–48
murder data, 86, 88
police officer death data, 134
SGFS relation to, 168
study of success of, 67
Brisman, Julissa, 86
Brody, Peter, 103–115
Bureau of Alcohol, Tobacco, Firearms and Explosives (BATF),
42–43, 52–53
Bush (George) administration
background check support,
210
ban weapons changes, 186
caving in to NRA by, 180–181
gun crime increases during,
138
gun show private sales opposition, 210
individual right viewpoint, 18

NICS signing/implementation, 139–140

Bush v. Gore, 201

Byrdsong, Ricky, 104, 108–110

C

Calderón, Felipe, 52

Can Gun Control Work? (Jacobs), 67

Canada
backfiring of gun ban, 93
Crime Prevention Ottawa report, 124
Firearms and Violent Crime report, 118
gangs in Ottawa, 120
preventive measure analysis, 124–125
social/cultural forces in, 117–118
suicide rate stability, 64, 65
youth risk factors, 123–124

Center for Gun Policy Research (Johns Hopkins University), 101

Centers for Disease Control and Prevention (CDC), 31–32, 33, 148

Centerwall, Brandon, 33

Chicago schools gun violence, 88–89

Children
deaths from gun violence, 27, 70, 71–72
Eddie Eagle Guidesafe Program, 76–79
epidemic myths, 76
FBI death data, 34
gun violence threats to, 69–73

Children's Defense Fund (CDF)
gun violence vs. children report, 70, 71
safety measures called for by, 72

Cho, Seung-Hui, 22, 27, 82, 128–130, 162
See also Virginia Tech University

City of New York, 207–213

Clarkson, Lana, 86

Clinton, Bill, 210

Coaching Your Kids in the Game of Life (Byrdsong), 109

Coalition to Stop Gun Violence, 192

College campuses
concealed weapons removal, 155–166
Coulter's opinion about, 22–23
examples of campus shooters, 162
homicide rate (2001 study), 156–157
law-abiding vs. non-law-abiding citizens, 161–163
myth of deterrence, 159–161
risks of concealed handguns, 157–159
See also Virginia Tech University

Columbine High School shooting, 51, 87, 95, 223

Community Service and Youth Activities Division (NSC), 77

Concealed-carry of guns
deterrence effect, 172–173
intellectual debate about, 170–171
laws about, 34–35, 149

in national parks, as dangerous, 185–188

in national parks, as safe, 179–184

overblown concerns (opinion), 171–172

statistics, 173–175

Congress (U.S.)

Armed Career Criminal Act, 16

Gun Control Act, 15, 16, 47, 82, 134

gun violence prevention attempts, 70

statistics used by, 52

Constitution (U.S.)

Bill of Rights, 38–39

Fifteenth/Nineteenth Amendments, 195–196

Thirteenth Amendment, 38

See also Second Amendment; Supreme Court

Cook, Philip, 19

"Cop-killing" handguns, 47

Coulter, Ann, 22–23

Counter-Strike video game, 128

Crime Prevention Ottawa report (2008), 124

"Crimes and Misconceptions" (Smith), 92

Cruikshank, United States v., 38

Cruikshank, William, 38

D

Davis, Joseph Q., 121

Deakins, Jacob, 30–40

Delaware Couny Daily Times, 221–225

Denying Firearms and Explosives to Dangerous Terrorists Act, 140

Detroit Free Press article, 35–36

Diaz, Tom, 41–49

District of Columbia v. Heller, 14–15, 19, 36, 58, 135, 148, 153, 201–202, 202–204, 204–205

Domestic violence

by Benjamin Smith, 105, 107

Brady Law and, 138–139

Florida statistics, 163

gun ownership and, 174

Lautenberg Amendment, 135

by Michael Kennedy, 160–161

NICS and, 209

by Randy Edward Hayes, 134

reduction attempts, 18–19

by Richard Poplawski, 112

Dorélien, Astrid, 103–115

Drug cartels in Mexico

border disputes with U.S., 44–45

disagreements between cartels, 227

exaggerated weapons data, 50

gun's purchased from U.S., 41–42

ineffectiveness in disarming, 227, 229

military-style weapons used by, 42–43

U.S. policy gaps and, 43–44

Drug trafficking organizations (DTOs), 43–44

Duncan, Arne, 88

Dziewanski, Dariusz, 116–126

E

Economist news magazine, 23

Eddie Eagle GunSafe Program, 76–79

Edelman, Marian Wright, 69–73

Elder, Larry, 184
Emanuel, Rahm, 140
"The Embarrassing Second Amendment" (Levinson), 18
Emerson, United States v., 18
Enforcement Acts (1876), 38
Enter the Babylon System (Pearce), 118–119
Episodes of gun violence
    abortion provider murder, 110–111
    Army recruitment station attack, 111–112
    Benjamin Smith shooting spree, 106–110
    Chicago schools, 88–89
    Columbine High School shooting, 51, 87, 95, 223
    Holocaust Memorial Museum shooting, 104, 105, 113–114
    Jewish Community Center shootings, 104, 108
    Markoff murder of Brisman, 86
    New Life Church, 35
    Omaha shopping mall, 35
    Pennsylvania mass police shooting, 112–113
    Ricky Byrdsong murder, 104, 108–110
    shooting of Jordan Manners, 92
    Spector murder of Clarkson, 86
    William Long murder, 111–112
    Won-Joo Yoon murder, 104, 108–109
    Youth With A Mission Training center, 35
    See also Virginia Tech University (college shooting)

Espinosa, Patricia, 49
Everitt, Ladd, 134

F

Face the Nation (CBS news show), 51, 54
"Facts About Kids and Guns," 72
FBI
    D.C. 2006 murder rate data, 152
    Joint Terrorism Task Force, 111
    justifiable firearm homicide data, 165–166
    murder investigations/arrest data, 191
    U.S. counties ownership data, 34
Fear tactics, 31–32
Federal Election Commission, 95
Federal Firearms License (FFL), 47, 208–209
Feinstein, Dianne, 52, 185–188
Fiessinger, Donald, 107–108
Fifteenth Amendment, 195–196
"Fire sale" loophole, 146
Firearm Owners Protection Act (FOPA, 1986), 16, 143
Firearms and Violent Crime report (Canada), 118
Firearms Discharge Report (NYC Police Dept.), 164
Flores, Robert, 162
Fox, James Alan, 23
Fox News, 52–53
Fraser Forum, 64
Frenkil, Steven D., 163

G

Gangs in Canada (Ottawa), 120
Goddard, Andrew, 25–29
Gostin, Lawrence, 148, 152
Great Britain, banning of weapons, 93
Greenberg, Paul, 55
Gun Ban for Individuals Convicted of a Misdemeanor Crime of Domestic Violence (Lautenberg Amendment), 19, 134–135
Gun Control Act (1968), 15, 16, 47, 82, 134
Gun control advocates/advocacy
  Ann Coulter vs., 22–23
  AWB efforts, 227
  exaggerations by, 50, 53
  gun lobby vs., 17–18
  Lautenberg Amendment and, 19, 134–135
  on lax gun control laws, 169
  opinions on purchases of guns, 101
  Second Amendment vs., 17–18, 193, 228
  Violence Policy Center, 44, 88, 163, 224
"Gun Control Fact-Sheet" (Gun Owners Foundation), 76
Gun-Free School Zone laws, 22–23
Gun-free zones, 22–23, 35
Gun-hate connection, 104–106
Gun industry in the U.S.
  Brady Law relation to, 138
  employee screening proposals, 145
  lack of purchase limitations, 48
  NRA relation to, 95

  oversight lacks, 49
  role of, 44–45
  structure of, 47
  weapon design choices, 42–43
Gun Owners Foundation, 76
Gun Owners of America (GOA), 17, 22, 135
Gun ownership
  background checks, 97
  benefits of, 34–36
  Brady Campaign views on, 136–146
  disposal of weapons, 87
  gun violence connection to, 30–34
  hate connection, 104–106
  home protection data, 37
  laws as deterrent to crimes, 147–154
  19th-century cases, 39
  research misconceptions, 32–33
  safety issues, 150
  success linked to, 122–123
  suicide and, increased risks, 57–62
  suicide and, non-increased risks, 63–68
  See also Second Amendment
"Gun Rights Debate" (Jost), 195
Gun shows
  availability of guns at, 217
  background checks as unnecessary, 214–220
  Brady Campaign extension to, 138
  case for closing loopholes, 207–213
  hate group attraction to, 105
Gun violence
  "average day" data, 27
  cultural connections, 101

gun ownership connection to, 30–34
laws as deterrent to crimes, 147–154
Mayors (of cities) against, 70
medical costs of, 88
popular culture influence, 116–126
prevention campaign, 88
preventive measures, 124–125
pro-organization policy promotion of, 94–97
protests against, 99–100
reduction suggestions, 138–141
research misconceptions, 32–33
seriousness of problem, 25–29
as symptom of social problems, 98–102
U.S. culture promotion of, 127–131
U.S. data related to, 137–138
youth connection to, 118–119
See also Brady Campaign to Prevent Gun Violence
"Gun Violence Overview" (Brady Campaign to Prevent Gun Violence), 27
"Guns, Fear, the Constitution, and the Public's Health" (Wintemute), 31
Gura, Alan, 18–19

H

Halbrook, Stephen, 18
Halder, Biswanath, 162
Hale, Matthew, 106
Hammer, Marion P., 76, 78
Harvard Journal of Law & Public Policy, 32

Hate groups, 103–106, 114
Hawaii firearms fatalities, 97
Hayes, Mary Ann, 134
Hayes, Randy Edward, 134–135
Hayes, Robert, 108
Hayes, United States v., 19
Healy, Steven, 23
Heller, District of Columbia v., 14–15, 19, 36, 58, 135, 148, 153, 201–202, 202–204
Helmke, Paul, 83
See also Brady Campaign to Prevent Gun Violence
Hemenway, David, 57–62, 72, 148, 151
Henigan, Dennis, 19
Herbert, Bob, 85–88, 115
Hezbollah terrorist group, 96
Hoar, William P., 50–56
Holder, Eric
assault weapon support ban, 54, 141, 224, 228
background check support, 138–140
on gun show loophole, 138
on terrorist gun examples, 140
Holocaust Memorial Museum shooting, 104, 105, 113–114
Homeland Security Department (DHS), 104
Homicides (from guns)
by adolescents, 118
bans and increase of, 93
black male/Hispanic data, 137
Brady Law influence on, 67, 138
justifiable homicides, 110–111, 165
NEJM article, 150
at postsecondary institutions, 155–157, 160

race/ethnicity data, 100
suicides vs., 32, 57, 58, 66–67
U.S. 2005 data, 165
Honberg, Ron, 84
Hoover, William J., 42, 53
Horwitz, Joshua, 192

I

Immigration and Customs En-
forcement (U.S., ICE), 53
Inhofe, James, 53–54
Injury Epidemiology and Control
(CDC), 32
"Inside Gun Shows" (Wintemute),
211
Intentional Injuries Section
(CDC), 32
Internet gun exchanges, 48
Interstate gun sales, 16
IRA (Irish Republican Army), 96

J

Jacobs, James B., 151
Jeunesse, William La, 52
Jewish Community Center shoot-
ings, 104, 108
    See also Holocaust Memorial
    Museum shooting
Joint Terrorism Task Force (of
FBI), 111
Jost, Kenneth, 195
Journal of Emergency Nursing On-
line, 77
Journal of the American Medical
Association (JAMA), 147–149,
152, 154
Judicial activism and the Second
Amendment, 200–206

K

Kates, Don B., 32–33, 63–68, 193–
199
Kazmierczak, Steven, 162
Keane, Lawrence G., 191
Kelly, Ray, 164
Kennedy, John F., 15
Kennedy, Robert F., 15
Kill the Best Gentiles (Von Brunn),
113
King, Martin Luther, Jr., 15
King, Peter, 140
Kleck, Gary, 23
Kmiec, Douglas, 201
Ku Klux Klan, 38
    See also Cruikshank, William

L

La Pierre, Wayne, 54
Lautenberg, Frank, 140
Lautenberg Amendment (Gun Ban
for Individuals Convicted of a
Misdemeanor Crime of Domes-
tic Violence), 19, 134–135
Legislation
    Armed Career Criminal Act,
    16
    blocking commonsense laws,
    96–97
    evidence of success, 97
    Gun Control Act, 15, 16, 47,
    82
    NICS, 17, 83, 139–140, 162
    NICS (1988), 17, 83
    weakening of laws, 95–96
    See also Brady Law; Constitu-
    tion (U.S.); Supreme Court
    decisions
Levin, Jack, 23

Levinson, Sanford, 18

Levy, Robert A., 147–154

Libertarian beliefs about concealed weapons, 179–184

Lindenberger, Michael, 51

Lo, Wayne, 162

Long, William, 111–112

Lott, John R., 34, 37, 52, 90–93

Lott, Maxim, 52

M

Maine firearms fatalities, 97

Mangan, Tom, 44

Manners, Jordan, 92

Markoff, Philip, 86

Mass police shooting, Pennsylvania, 112–113

Massachusetts firearms fatalities, 97

A Matter of Interpretation: Federal Courts and the Law (Scalia), 18

Mauser, Gary, 32–33, 64

McDonald, Andrew J., 192

McLelland, Sandra J., 163

Media

    violent images promoted by, 128–129

    Virginia Tech University commentary, 82

Medical costs of gun violence, 88

Menino, Thomas, 70

Mental health groups, 83–84

Mexico

    drug cartel use of guns, 42–43

    DTOs in, 43–44

    gun smuggling into, 228–229

    gun violence exaggerations, 50–56

    guns from U.S. in, 41–49

    reasons for increased violence, 43–44

Michigan Association of Chiefs of Police, 36

Microstamping law (California), 192

Military-style weapons

    ease in buying, 41, 45, 82–83, 95–96, 225

    import limitation attempts, 49

    loopholes in ownership, 114

    Mexico drug cartel use of, 41

    Mexico drug cartel's use of, 42–43

    ownership limitation attempts, 221–222

Miller, David, 91

Miller, Matthew, 57–62, 148, 151

Miller, Michael, 103–115

Miller, United States v., 14

Million Mom March, 25

Mills, Mark, 128–129

More Guns, Less Crime (Lott), 52

Moritz, E. Stewart, 19

Muhammad, Abdulhakim Mujahid, 111–112

N

National Academy of Sciences (U.S.), 33

National Alliance on Mental Illness, 84

National Association of School Safety and Law Enforcement Officers, 77

National Council to Control Handguns, 16

National Instant Criminal Background Check System (NICS, 1998), 17, 83, 139–140, 162

National Park Rangers Lodge of the Fraternal Order of Police, 187

National Park Service employees group, 187

National parks
danger of concealed weapons, 185–188
safety of concealed weapons, 179–184

National Parks Conservation Association, 187

National Rifle Association (NRA), 22
admission of violence problem, 22
on armed vs. unarmed citizens, 118
assault weapon data, 54
Bush's caving in to, 180–181
campus concealed weapons support, 156
gun industry relation to, 95
inflammatory rhetoric by, 115
Institute for Legislative Action of, 74–79
NICS relation to, 17
origins of, 16
"slippery slope" strategy, 205
support of specific legislation, 83

National Safety Council (NSC), 77

National School Public Relations, 77

National Security Threat Levels, 28

National Sheriffs' Association (NSA), 77

National Shooting Sports Foundation, 191

NBC airing of Cho's rants, 130

Neo-Nazi shooting spree, 106–110

New England firearms fatalities, 97

New England Journal of Medicine (NEJM), 31–32, 147–152

New Life Church shootings, 35

Newell, William, 44, 53

NICS. See National Instant Criminal Background Check System

Nineteenth Amendment (U.S. Constitution), 195–196

O

Obama, Barack
assault weapon ban efforts, 55
background check support, 210
on gun show loophole, 138
gun show private sales opposition, 210
Mexico visit statement, 52

O'Carroll, Patrick, 32

Officer Down-Assault Weapons and the War on Law Enforcement (VPC study), 224

Omaha shopping mall shooting, 35

O'Reilly, Bill, 131

Oswald, Lee Harvey, 15

P

Pearce, Christian, 118–119, 124–125

Pennsylvania mass police shooting, 112–113

Phoenix Field Division (ATF), 44

Poeun, Chris, 92

Police Athletic League (PAL), 77

Police shooting in Pennsylvania, 112–113

Poplawski, Richard, 112–113

Popular culture and gun violence, 116–126

Pratt, Larry, 22

"Protect Children, Not Guns" (Children's Defense Fund), 70

R

Race Against Hate (Byrdsong memorial), 110

Reagan, Ronald, 186

RED security threat level, 28

Rice, Condolezza, 48–49

Right-to-carry laws, 34

Right-wing hate groups, 106

Risk factors for youth, 123–124

Robertson v. Baldwin, 38

Rodgers, Dennis, 123

Rosenthal, John E., 94–97

Rush, Bobby Lee, 55–56

S

Safety programs for children, 74–79

Sarukh'n, Arturo, 51

Saturday Night Specials (guns), 107

Scalia, Justice Antonin, 14, 18, 201

SCCC. See Students for Concealed Carry on Campus

Schieffer, Bob, 51

Schoolchildren shooting victims, 17

Schwan, Clair, 179–184

Scott v. Sandford, 36

Second Amendment (U.S. Constitution), 14–18
  Brady Law vs., 134–135
  in the courts, 36–38
  judicial activism and, 200–206
  limitations of rights, 95
  minority individual rights interpretations, 16
  private gun ownership guarantee, 193–199
  public health vs., 153
  Robertson v. Baldwin and, 38
  supporters vs. opposers, 53–54
  Supreme Court on, 18, 38–40, 106
  See also District of Columbia v. Heller

Second Amendment Foundation, 37

Self-defense
  myth of, 165–167
  preparation for, in national parks, 184

September 11, 2001 terrorist attack, 25, 28

Sheptycki, James, 119

Shields, Pete, 15–16

Smith, Benjamin, 105, 106–110
  See also Holocaust Memorial Museum shooting

Smith, Jordan Michael, 92

Smugglers/smuggling of guns
  ATF prevention efforts, 48
  Florida conviction for, 217
  lack of success catching, 93
  Mexico as prime target for, 228–229
  prevention problems, 46
  prosecutions for, 44–45
  sentencing proposals, 120
  U.S. firearms market and, 46

Soviet Union, fear tactics, 31
Spector, Phil, 86
Stabbing of Chris Poeun, 92
Stephen, Andrew, 127–131
Stevens, Justice John Paul, 14
Steyn, Mark, 128, 131
Students for Concealed Carry on
  Campus (SCCC), 156, 167–178
Students for Gun Free Schools
  (SGFS), 155–166, 168
Success images with guns, 122–
  123
Suicide
    accidental shootings vs., 88
    analysis of data, 151
    children and teen data, 71–72
    college campus data, 158–160,
      171–172
    firearm ban and, 32
    global data, 64–65
    gun availability, increase of,
      32, 57–62
    gun availability, non-increase
      of, 63–68
    individual states/gun owner-
      ship, 60, 151
    misleading claims about,
      66–68
    NEJM article, 148, 150
    reduction through gun con-
      trol, 33
    white vs. black rates, 71
"The Suicide and Gun-Deaths
  Fraud" article (Kates), 64
Supreme Court
    Lautenberg Amendment
      backed by, 135
    Second Amendment view of,
      18, 38–40, 106
    See also individual Supreme
      Court decisions

T

Taney, Roger, 36
Third Way gun control group, 83
Thirteenth Amendment (U.S.
  Constitution), 38
Thornton, Billy, 77
Time magazine, 51
Trafficking of guns, 107

U

United States
    ATF Bureau, 42–43, 141–145
    "average" gun violence data,
      27
    CDC agencies/conclusions,
      31–32, 33
    civilian gun ownership, 87
    cultural promotion of gun
      violence, 127–131
    Gun Control Act, 15, 16, 47,
      82, 134
    gun control policy gaps,
      43–44
    gun death ranking, 142
    Immigration and Customs
      Enforcement, 53
    military-style weapons mar-
      keting, 42–43
    National Academy of Sciences,
      33
    National Security Threat Lev-
      els, 28
    9/11/2001 terrorist attack, 25,
      28
    regulation/enforcement gaps,
      45–47
    role of gun industry in, 44–45
    state concealed weapons data,
      149
    suicide vs. murder rates, 65

system-wide weaknesses in, 47–49
Violence Policy Center, 44
See also Congress; Constitution (U.S.); Supreme Court
United States v. Cruikshank, 38
United States v. Emerson, 18
United States v. Hayes, 19
United States v. Miller, 14

V

Vermont firearms fatalities, 97
Video games and violence, 121, 128
Violence Policy Center (VPC), 44, 88, 163, 224
Violence Prevention Research Program (UC Davis), 211
Virginia Tech University (college shooting), 22
    ease in purchasing gun, 82–83, 95
    Goddard/son's experience, 26–29
    Judge Barnett's ruling, 82
    media commentary about, 82
    murder-suicide relation of shooter, 160
    post-shooting action by SCCC, 156, 167
    See also Cho, Seung-Hui
Von Brunn, James, 113–114

W

Waller, Irvin, 120
Warrick, Steven, 226–229
Washington, D.C. murder rata, 91–92
Washington Post newspaper, 52
Webster, Daniel, 101
White supremacy. *See* Poplawski, Richard; Smith, Benjamin
Wintemute, Garen J., 211
    gun ownership/violence assertions, 32
    New England Journal article, 31
    public shooting focus, 35
World Church of the Creator right-wing hate group, 106

Y

Yildiz, Ugur "Mike," 146
Yoon, Won-Joon, 104, 108–109
Youth With A Mission Training center shooting, 35

Z

"Zebra" murders (San Francisco), 15–16

.